Kaiser Karl

Raphaëlle Bacqué

Kaiser Karl

ACC ART BOOKS

© 2020 ACC Art Books Ltd
© Éditions Albin Michel – Paris 2019

ISBN: 978-1-78884-070-5

Originally published in French under the title *Kaiser Karl* by Éditions Albin Michel,
22 Rue Huyghens, 75014, Paris
This English edition published by ACC Art Books in 2020, by agreement with
Éditions Albin Michel

British Library Cataloguing-in-Publication Data
A catalogue record for this book is available from the British Library.

The author and publisher gratefully acknowledge the permission granted to
reproduce the copyright material in this book. Every effort has been made to trace
copyright holders and to obtain their permission for the use of copyright material.
The publisher apologises for any errors or omissions in the text and would be grateful
if notified of any corrections that should be incorporated in future reprints or
editions of this book.

English Edition
Translator: Caroline Beamish
Editor: Bryony Porter
Production: Craig Holden

Printed in Slovenia by DZS Grafik for
ACC Art Books Ltd., Woodbridge, Suffolk, IP12 4SD, UK

www.accartbooks.com

"One day, when I am old and have withdrawn from life, I shall live with my sofa and comfy armchairs and the table at which I used to draw and paint... and I shall sleep in my childhood bed."

Karl Lagerfeld

Preamble

No burial, no ceremony. No filing past the coffin. No tears – such an error of taste. "Rather than dying," said Lagerfeld, somewhat strangely, "I just want to disappear, like the animals in the forest…"

Nevertheless, plain clothes policemen and private security guards stand every fifteen metres along the hearse's route. A line of black limousines waits in front of the crematorium on Mont Valérien. Chauffeurs in narrow suits, models climbing the path in their very high heels, owners of brands scurrying along – it's like a funereal fashion week.

A few minutes earlier, a small group of intimate friends had gathered in front of the black, open coffin. Karl Lagerfeld lay inside, stretched out stiff on the white satin cushions, wearing his dark glasses, with powder in his hair. He would have hated being exposed in such a way, wearing his 'panoply' – the accessories that had, for so long, served as his mask – over the waxy complexion of a corpse. But such is the fate of the dead. Until this moment, Lagerfeld had reigned supreme over fashion, and neither his shareholders nor his collaborators had dared contradict him. Now he is gone, they are disobeying his orders already.

All the same, the directors of Chanel, who organised the ceremony, did not dare act with a completely free hand. Around two hundred people were invited, by invitation card as if to a party, but wreaths and flowers were banned. No mass, either. "Karl loved the solemn grandeur of a cathedral, but he was an atheist," whispers a female friend. The surroundings are grim and ugly. No grand scenery, none of the bouquets and lighting that provided the background to Lagerfeld's fashion shows during his final years.

In this half high-society, half down-to-earth gathering, the guests have been seated according to a subtle social hierarchy – one that in no way reflects the creation of a garment. In the front row: Alain Wertheimer, the owner of Chanel. The owner of LVMH, Bernard Arnault, sits on the other side of the aisle, accompanied by two of his children, Antoine and Delphine. Princess Caroline of Monaco is behind him, with Anna Wintour (the high priestess of fashion), Inès de la Fressange and Baptiste Giabiconi, Lagerfeld's favourite model. Florentine Pabst has arrived from Hamburg, Karl's birthplace – she is the couturier's oldest friend. In the crowd of those closest to him, Virginie Viard can just be made out: the designer who spent twenty years in the shadow of the master. Appointed as his successor some hours after his death, she does not yet dare emerge into the light.

Behind this assembly of celebrities, we finally find the head seamstresses of the workroom. They have spent hours upon hours down on one knee, sticking pins into fabulous fabrics. Only they know how much hard labour goes into making a light, loose-fitting blouse emerge from a roll of silk. Some weep – but only a handful attend the ceremony. Most of those who work in haute couture did not receive an invitation.

It is a strange event. Nothing recalls the dearly departed, except perhaps the lines by the French poet Catherine Pozzi that Lagerfeld translated into German (and which Princess Caroline chose as a reading, delivering the words in a perfect accent). That is the risk you take, when you refuse to think about death. The designer left no instructions – except a request for no funeral, and the following statement of the obvious, which rings out like a command: "When it's finished, it's finished!"

His death remained taboo until it happened, even on 19 February 2019, the Tuesday morning when he died in the American Hospital in Neuilly, at the age of eighty-five. He had been transferred there the day before, and though his bodyguard and trusted confidant, Sébastien Jondeau, stayed by his side, it seems his entourage were taken by surprise. Suddenly, the flourishing world of fashion was paralysed. It took several hours of confabulation in Rue Cambon before Lagerfeld's passing was made public – the death of the last emperor of fashion seemed like an act of sacrilege.

Some months earlier, I had begun to gather material for an article about him in *Le Monde*. I was met with suspicion: "It's not for an obituary, is it?" his collaborators enquired in alarm. Even the powerful Bernard Arnault

– the redoubtable boss of LVMH, with his chilly look of a shark gliding through deep water – vehemently confirmed that what Lagerfeld said was true. At Fendi, owned by LVMH, for whom 'Karl' had been designing the fur collection since 1965, the contract was 'for life'. Arnault scotched all rumours about Lagerfeld's successor with a single utterance: "I don't want to think about it. And anyway, we never discuss it. The only other case like Karl's is the case of the Pope, you know!"

Pope, emperor, *Kaiser* – and not a single biography... That's what struck me first. This man at the crossroads of power, money, the media and fashion remained a total secret. It could not be said, however, that his face, his appearance, or his accent were unknown. Some years earlier, when I found myself lost while reporting from the depths of China, I was helped by a peasant at the wheel of an old banger. His face was criss-crossed with wrinkles, he wore ancient blue overalls, and we spoke to each other in sign language. Pinned on to the lapel of his jacket was an incongruous gleaming badge. I immediately recognised the elegant silhouette, the dark glasses and white pony tail. And yet Lagerfeld, who had penetrated to the depths of the Chinese countryside, remained a mystery. Though he was recognised everywhere, he had managed to prevent people from ever knowing who he really was.

When we first met, Lagerfeld was on the defensive. After months of negotiation, he appeared one evening with his mittens, his rings – two or three on each finger – and a brooch by Suzanne Belperron pinned to his cravat. In short, he wore all the accessories of "the puppet whose strings I control," as he used to say. To demonstrate his goodwill – or perhaps to mislead me from the start – he removed his dark glasses. His gaze was brown, simultaneously sarcastic and gentle. Less alarming, anyway. He spoke with his characteristic rapid phrasing and aristocratic German accent, which anyone I interviewed later would immediately begin to imitate. But he soon destroyed my preconceptions: for three hours he showered me with delightful anecdotes, then concluded with a heartfelt cry: "At any rate, almost all the people who know my story are in the cemetery now…"

He was wrong. I met several who had crossed paths with this man before he became an actor completely submerged in his role. Many revealed only a single shred of the story. Others waited until his death to talk about him without fear. I had to gather these traces, reconsider the legend he had been creating over the past sixty years, and try to understand what had made this war-born scion of the German bourgeoisie a model of the luxury industries and the globalised world. Little by little, the puzzle came together.

1

My first trip was to Hamburg. Fourteen months before he died, when rumours of his illness were ebbing and flowing like the tide, Karl Lagerfeld wanted to organise a fashion show in the town of his birth. I left Paris in his wake.

In December 2017, it was exceptionally cold on the banks of the Elbe. Chanel had invited three thousand people to the Elbphilharmonie, where the cruise collection was to be shown; a large party was planned for later on the docks. Oddly enough, for two days Lagerfeld insisted that he was not leaving his hotel.

This was the first time the couturier had presented his dresses and suits in the town where he was born – but he warned from the start: "I am against travelling into my own past". He did not want this return to his origins to be interpreted: "To those who say that we have come full circle, shut up!" To pre-empt any inquisition, he criticised Angela Merkel so fiercely for her migration policy and her lack of dress sense that the mayor of Hamburg refused to come and welcome this local boy who was so unwilling to celebrate his origins. The press hardly dared ask him about his German youth. For my own part, I am not sure where to begin, so surprised was I by his reticence on the subject of his home country – this man who had always seemed so Prussian to me.

Lagerfeld had reserved tables for lunch at Jacob's, the restaurant whose shady terrace was painted in the 1920s by Max Liebermann, before the arrival of Nazism forced the artist to resign from the Academy of Arts in Berlin. The couturier invited friends and collaborators to dine beneath the crystal chandeliers of the dining room, the tall windows looking down on the river below. This was where he used to come on Sundays with his parents.

Lagerfeld handed me a photograph of his mother, Elisabeth, an elegant, middle-class woman wearing a double row of pearls, and another of his father. In his photograph, Otto Lagerfeld must be about forty years old. He sports an elegant tweed jacket, flannel trousers and large walking boots, like a man of the world who enjoys a bit of sport on the side. "A Weimar German," Lagerfeld said.

The big party organised by Lagerfeld was entirely conceived in the taste of the 1920s, with sailors in pea coats singing sailor songs, sausages to eat and beer to drink. The Germany he wanted to serve up to this gathering of people from all over the world was a replica of the pre-war period.

In the 1930s, the Lagerfelds lived in Blankenese, a suburb in the uplands above Hamburg. Their house was near Baurs Park, an area which has remained as green and tranquil as it was in Karl's childhood. From its highest points, the giant ships and barges can be seen slipping along the dark river Elbe. Otto Lagerfeld must have chosen this great industrial port deliberately – he spent the first years of his working life at sea, sailing first to Venezuela then the United States.

The family claim that Otto, born in 1889, witnessed the earthquake that ravaged San Francisco in 1906. The Great War of 1914-1918, which decimated the population of Europe, hardly touched him. "He was in Vladivostok," Karl said. Otto was there on business – the climax of his career in commerce. From here, the most eastern city in Europe, Otto introduced American Carnation evaporated milk to Russia, renaming it *Gvozdika* (Carnation) to better appeal to his market. He was just beginning to make money when the warning signs of the Russian Revolution caught him on the hop. From then on, in the eyes of the Lagerfelds, he was an adventurer as much as a businessman. His son was the only exception; he spoke severely of his father, as one might of an accountant.

In the many interviews granted to me by Karl Lagerfeld, he was always more willing to talk about his mother. Elisabeth Bahlmann, a divorcée from Prussia, was seventeen years younger than Otto when he married her in 1930 (himself a widower and father to little Thea). One thing strikes you when you look at these portraits: Karl inherited everything from his mother. He had the same brown eyes, so deep-set that they look almost black; the same thick hair and sensual lips that curl into an ironic smile. Was it Elisabeth, who gave him his taste for mystery and his manner of always juggling the truth?

"You can ask me about my childhood and about anything since I met your father," she said to Karl. "What happened in the middle is none of your business." 'In the middle' must mean her social origins, which she chose to hide. Before she married Otto, she was a lingerie saleswoman in Berlin – according to what Kurt Lagerfeld, Karl's cousin, told the English journalist Alicia Drake. In addition to being divorced – not an enviable position for a woman at that time – she must have been attractive and vibrant enough at thirty-two to have contracted a marriage that gained her entry to the wealthy bourgeoisie.

Returning to Hamburg in December 2017, followed by a flotilla of fashion editors, was like placing my foot on the shaky ground of the past. Since his rise to fame, Karl Lagerfeld had produced several versions of his past, each more extraordinary than the last. He told me about his family's lifestyle a thousand times – the cook for the dinners, the gardener in the park, the governess for the children. Elisabeth did not lift a finger in the house, or to help with her children's education. "She would say: 'One has to think of oneself first and foremost, so that other people can take care of one's nearest and dearest,'" Karl claimed. A woman from Berlin, who had fled to Hamburg in the Great War, was hired to give French lessons to Karl and his sisters: Martha-Christine, always called Christel, two years his senior; and Thea.

Lagerfeld always described himself as a very precocious child. He was born on 10 September 1933 and insisted that he could already read and write in German and speak adequate English and French at the age of five. He was 'a child of elderly parents'. Or was he ever a child at all? In the photos, standing up straight in his little suit, he looks as if he could launch into conversation just like any adult.

For years I have tried to find out what Otto did to escape the effects of Nazism during the Second World War, the destruction of Hamburg, the purges and the settling of scores once peace had returned. Did Karl ever ask him? His father recounted his adventures to the family over and over again – but not his compromises with the Nazi regime. Karl related how, in 1925, Otto wound down his business importing foodstuffs to join the American Milk Products Corporation. At the age of forty-five he created the German branch, Glücksklee, to manufacture evaporated milk. Rather than importing the milk, he started the concentration process in German factories, notably in Neustadt, about thirty kilometres from Lübeck.

"His ambition was focused entirely on maximising his profits," Karl assured me; he never allowed his father much of a role in his stories. If we are to believe him, the industrialist was always more interested in business than in politics. At that time, however, was it really possible to turn one's back on the upheavals of history?

In the early 1940s, the Prussian bourgeoisie seems to have lived much as usual in the suburb of Blankenese, even those who had sons at the Front. The German press only reported the Wehrmacht's victories. Nevertheless, on Mittelweg, where the offices of Glücksklee-Milch were situated at number 36, more and more flats stood empty:

apartments that had belonged to the Jewish middle classes of Hamburg. These Jews were so assimilated that most did not believe Hitler's arrival to be a threat.

Mittelweg still stands, the town's throbbing heart of commerce. Seventy-five years later, your toe stubs continually against small gilded cobbles fixed in the ground. The 'Stolpersteine' – literally 'stumbling blocks' – were installed during the 1990s as memorial markers. One stone equals one person deported. Could Otto really have been unaware of how many of his neighbours had disappeared – diplomats, lawyers and doctors, all replaced after 1941 by the National-Socialist nomenklatura who moved into their empty flats?

By this time, Karl's father was in his fifties: too old to be called up. This was a stroke of luck in a country where eighteen million men were at the Front, of whom five and a half million died and the others returned defeated and shamed. Because he wished to own a second home, but also undoubtedly because he had witnessed the effects of the Revolution in Russia, one year after Hitler's arrival in 1934, Otto bought a property forty kilometres north-west of Hamburg, very near the small resort of Bad Bramstedt. It was not an opportunity to be missed. The financial crisis of the 1930s had ruined the German landowners who until then had held sway over the provinces, and Otto was not the only member of the republican Hamburg business community to buy land when it became available.

Karl Lagerfeld often made drawings of his childhood home – the only home he really remembered. In his sketches, Bissenmoor looks like any one of the aristocratic estates scattered all over Schleswig-Holstein. The huge white house dates from 1900, with a large terrace, a balcony and a neo-classical façade. A large paved carriage sweep lies at the front of the house, as well as a flower bed and 3,000 hectares of forest.

The house was first turned into a restaurant and then an old people's home. Today, it has finally fallen into ruins – I could not find a single trace of it. But the surroundings still offer fine rural landscapes, refreshed by sea breezes from the North Sea in the west and the Baltic in the east. The village of Bad Bramstedt has grown, but still contains only 15,000 inhabitants. The landscape retains the freshness of the meadows. The impression given by the many canals and rivers that criss-cross the greensward is of mirrors laid out on the grass.

From the mid-1930s, when war was threatening, Otto scouted round for local farms which, in case of war, could keep him supplied with milk. Young Karl was seven in 1940, and may have been unaware that a war was raging: "I have no memory of seeing my parents anxious, but they probably avoided talking about politics," he said, brushing my question aside.

Otto was far too experienced not to realise the danger. He spoke perfect English, French and a bit of Russian, enough to follow the news from the Front. In 1942 he decided to remove his family from the port of Hamburg, a strategic town in times of war. It had become dangerous, and Elisabeth and the children would be safer in Bad Bramstedt. For the girls, the couple thought the simplest expedient would be to enrol Thea and Christel in a boarding school a few miles from the village – but little Karl stayed with his mother, attending the Jürgen-Fuhlendorf, a small private school in the village. He was not yet ten years old and already felt like an exile, so far from the city.

When I asked him what he recalled of his youth, he directed me to *The White Ribbon*, a 2009 film by the Austrian director Michael Haneke. Sublime countryside populated by a cast of chilling characters – is this really what he thought of his childhood village?

When Karl pictured himself at the age of ten, he remembered first a feeling of absolute solitude. Life was so sluggish in this green rural landscape, where he seems to have never found a single friend. In his school photographs, he looks unlike anyone else. While all the other boys wear thick slipovers over their shirts, Karl stands out in a jacket with huge lapels and a cravat, his fringe worn long over his forehead. All the other boys adopted a shorter style that had been in fashion since the Nazis came to power: a close cut on the neck with a few longer locks of hair on top. Karl looks like a city-dweller and a dandy, out of place in this little village where life is lived under the stress of war.

A number of his slightly older neighbours enrolled in the Hitler Youth, as was obligatory from the age of fourteen. Dozens of boys in black shorts and khaki shirts organised walks and archery competitions every day, cultivating the healthy body extolled by the Nazi regime. How could Karl befriend them? He did not know how to climb trees or kick a football. It was a loneliness he remembered with relief later on: the impression of having always remained apart. However, he also developed a violent desire to escape his solitude.

Life in Bad Bramstedt was evidently safe enough for young Karl. In fact, this chaotic period had one wonderful advantage: he and his mother lived in very close intimacy. Otto was completely preoccupied by the fate of his factories, threatened by bombardments. In Neustadt, he even had to spend several days in prison – "he denounced someone who wanted to take over from him," Lagerfeld told me – and was struggling to keep milk production going; the milk fed the civilian population as well as the army.

As far back as he can remember, Karl saw himself as a little king, the object of everyone's attention. The family lived on a grander scale than their neighbours, with a gardener, a cook and a maid. But it was Karl who made an impression on the other children. From among his former classmates, I was only able to find one charming old lady, Ursula Scheube. Oh yes, she could certainly remember this small boy, "so different" from the rest. The child she described did not conform to the conventions of the time. Ursula saw him "drawing constantly, surrounded by boys of his age who were playing out of doors. He coloured during lessons, during break or on the doorstep of his parents' house."

Karl had to be self-confident – "arrogant and snobbish," he said later – to distinguish himself from the other boys who were lining up to join the uniformed, militarised mass of the Hitlerjugend. Karl was astonishingly over-confident sometimes, sure of his supremacy. Even his French teacher had to surrender to him. "He was fat and hunched and I was endlessly correcting his very mediocre pronunciation," Lagerfeld claimed, before adding: "I found it humiliating to be a child, a second-class citizen, when I felt so superior."

Though little Karl was more cherished, he was also more feminine than the tearaway boys surrounding him. In the adult world, this was a danger, a 'flaw' that could lead to deportation. As a child, Karl could count on his mother to defend him against teasing and prejudice. One day his class teacher took it upon himself to wipe Karl's face vigorously with his handkerchief, protesting that he was wearing lipstick. Elisabeth wrote a letter to the school expressing her dismay, and as the Lagerfelds were important folk, the teacher had to apologise.

He later recounted how he once asked, "What is a homosexual?" Oh, how well he remembered his mother's reply! "It's like having a particular hair colour, nothing more. What can it matter to civilised people?"

'What can it matter?' That is the way Karl summed up his life during the war: segregated from the tumult surrounding him. The provinces in the East lived as if they were in no danger. German planes could sometimes be seen flying over this sparkling countryside with its bracing sea breezes, and Allied planes circled the harbours and factories – but it was possible to feel far removed from the conflict that was rending Europe.

"I saw nothing of the war," – so Karl assured me emphatically on several occasions. I had to press him to acknowledge that he could remember the great bombing campaign over Hamburg. From 24 July to 3 August 1943, the British and American air forces loosed 10,000 tons of incendiary napalm bombs over the Hanseatic port and the east of the city, where the working classes lived. Hamburg was the first German city to be attacked by the Allies in an operation named 'Gomorrah'; it certainly resembled the divine destruction described in the Book of Genesis.

Over a radius of fifty kilometres, Germans gazed with horror at the flames and clouds of ash. "Yes, I saw the red sky and the aeroplanes," Karl admits. "We went up on a platform to look at the fires in the distance." Those same fires killed more than 40,000 people and destroyed over 80 per cent of this city, the place of Lagerfeld's birth.

It was not only Nazism that Karl forced himself to forget. It was also the anarchy that followed. The hundreds of thousands of refugees who fled the advance of the Red Army in the East – and the ambiguities after the war.

In 1945, Otto was sixty-five years old and could have retired. But polyglot, energetic German businessmen like him were scarce and he fearlessly pursued his career. The Hamburg archives were destroyed by fire, and the post-war purges were relatively mild, as this area lay under British administration. Everyone turned a blind eye to the fact that the Nazi administration had allowed Otto to continue as director of Glücksklee throughout the war – despite the fact that the company was classified, as a subsidiary of an American firm, as belonging to an enemy state. All this information is shrouded in the absolute silence that surrounds the 1940s.

Sixty-five years later, when he was admired the world over, Karl Lagerfeld revisited the city, but had no desire to return to his past. He was German, but absent from German history. I should have realised at the outset that it was from that moment that he began redesigning his life.

How did Karl persuade his parents to let him leave Germany at the age of nineteen? He had not yet taken his school leaving exam, but had mastered English and French. This was enough to start a new life. Thousands of young people planned to leave their country; Germany lay in ruins after the war, crushed by the shame of Nazism. It took little to convince Otto that his future lay elsewhere.

Karl's sister Christel also left, emigrating to the United States, where she soon found a husband and settled in Seattle. Karl swore by Paris. It seemed to him that only in the French capital could he make a clean break with the inhabitants of rural Hamburg he had come to hate. With his already well-developed superiority complex, his greatest wish was to escape provincialism.

Elisabeth showed her son's sketches to the director of the School of Fine Art in Hamburg. She liked literature and music, but Karl was undeniably most gifted at drawing. Hundreds of his sketches survive, made with a confident hand. "Caricatures of country children, portraits of friends and of my parents," Karl told me. The director spotted the signs of a young man with a definite interest in clothes, rather than a future artist. This didn't matter. When Elisabeth told her children that "Hamburg is the gateway to the world, but only the gateway – so get out!", no-one found any good reason to contradict her.

2

Karl always sat facing the door in the Café de Flore. It would have been difficult not to notice him, with his cashmere coat lying on the banquette and his lustrous brown hair cut like James Dean, as he scrutinised the neighbouring tables with a myopic gaze.

He thought he would stifle in Germany, now the object of worldwide hatred. So here he was in Paris, dazzled by the novelty of it all: a young dandy sat on the red seats of a café in the city's throbbing heart. No more war, no more ruins. The hungry, dirty peasants, the scarred cities – in 1952 he left it all behind.

Otto Lagerfeld retained the affluence enjoyed by the businessmen of the Hanseatic League, and he was generous. He financed all of Karl's needs, and more: the student hostel in the Rue de la Sorbonne and half a dozen suits from his personal tailor. In the Paris of the 1950s, where ration cards had only just been abolished, these suits turned the heads of passers-by.

I spent a long time wondering why Karl's father made such infrequent appearances in his son's memories. "I blame myself for not being nicer to him," Lagerfeld let slip. This probably stemmed from the secret blame and unexpressed anger which, at the time, undermined relations between Germans and their children. While living in Paris, Karl lunched only occasionally with this virile, deceptively indifferent man who continued to travel all over Europe. When they met, they would talk about Hamburg, where the port had resumed its activities, and about neighbours in the countryside – but almost never about the war.

"I know nothing about my parents' past," Lagerfeld told me one day. "Which means there is a past, but I know nothing about it. It's not my business. Anyway, I am happy to have no children; it spares me this kind of interrogation."

Was he thinking about the years when he tried to re-invent his genealogy? During the 1950s, Karl knew everything and nothing at the same time. Or rather, he was keen to doctor the truth. During those early interviews, I was sometimes distracted by how his autobiographical stories kept changing – but this may have been because he was trying to invent a non-German past for his father at the time. Or perhaps, he wanted him to be one of those Germans with no links to the war, who spent his time between the fairy-tale castles of Ludwig II of Bavaria and Goethe's library at his house in Weimar. An aristocrat sheltered by their education, like Erich von Stroheim in his surgical collar (who, since Jean Renoir's *La Grande Illusion*, was never really seen as the enemy).

It was then that Karl learned to steer conversation in order to avoid being questioned. It became second nature. What other man of twenty knew, as he did, how to skilfully manipulate anecdotes when the conversation threatened to return to wartime shortages, sons dead in combat and dishonest compromises on both sides – all subjects that still weighed heavily on people's minds? Even when Karl met a compatriot, he avoided any level of familiarity that might lead to questions about his past.

Once, a few years after his arrival in Paris, during a dinner at the residence of the countess Nicole de Blégiers, he met the couturier Azzedine Alaïa and his partner, Christoph von Weyhe. Von Weyhe was a few years younger than Karl and also came from Hamburg. Even better, his father, born into an aristocratic family from Schleswig-Holstein, owned acres and acres of pasture, along with herds of cows whose milk had supplied Otto Lagerfeld's factories. Von Weyhe had heard his father tell him over and over again: "Otto's son is in Paris; you should go and see him."

Von Weyhe had experienced the chaos of war far more than Karl. His mother, the daughter of a rich, aristocratic family, owned land near Halle, further east, where the family escaped to after the bombing of Hamburg. This was where the Red Army found them in 1945. Christoph von Weyhe was only seven, but can still remember the red star on the back of the jacket of the Russian officer who came to the door of their manor house and told them "The property is requisitioned and your lands have been redistributed. Tomorrow we are taking you to a refugee camp." By then, his father was a prisoner of the Americans, and his elder brother, called up in 1945 (when Hitler was in desperate straits), was in a Russian camp in Czechoslovakia. The moment the back of the Russian commandant was turned, Frau Von Weyhe took her children and one small suitcase and returned to Hamburg. To the West.

Christoph von Weyhe's career was almost the same as Karl's, although he was five years younger. Paris, then art school, after which he met Alaïa – a designer Karl did not like much. As two German exiles in Paris, Von Weyhe and Lagerfeld could have been friends, but Karl was far too busy re-inventing his past. A German, and the son of a friend of his father, posed far too great a risk of exposure.

Sixty years later, Christoph von Weyhe recalls the dinner where he was on the receiving end of Karl's small talk for the first time: "He spoke only of the house his parents had just bought in Baden-Baden, leading us to believe that he was from an aristocratic background; it might even have been Swedish!" Such whirling, well-informed and lightweight conversation. It was the start of the smoke screens that Karl crafted around himself with such expertise.

Imagine the hard work it took for Karl to obliterate his origins. In Paris, people still referred to the Germans as '*les Boches*'. Even the intellectuals and actresses who came to the Café de Flore to lunch on fried eggs would still allude to the '*Schleus*' and to '*Fritz*'. The conflict was only just over, and memories of the Occupation were very much alive.

All the smartest places in the capital bore the marks of the Occupation. The Hôtel Majestic in the Avenue Kléber had been home to the German military high command. The Lutetia to the Abwehr, the Ritz to the Luftwaffe. Various military governors had lived in the Hôtel Meurice. The Kommandantur held sway over the corner of Rue du 4-Septembre and the Avenue de l'Opéra; the Propagandastaffel were located in 52 Avenue des Champs-Élysées; and the German ambassador to France, Otto Abetz, in 78 Rue de Lille. As for Karl? He was learning to be a citizen of the world.

The waiters at Flore joked about the '*Frigolins*' ('Jerries'). Most of the Parisians with whom Karl mixed had only one wish: to rise above the 1940s. Otherwise, they made the Occupation the subject of derision. Bourvil and Gabin crossing the city to buy black market hams, in the comedy-drama *La Traversée de Paris* – that was the stuff of cinema. The Germans? You're joking!

Karl, however, was still on his guard. He had practised enunciating the word '*boche*' in a careless way. He seldom admitted to coming from Hamburg. When he had to order Frankfurter sausages ("a childhood weakness," he claimed) he pronounced the name in the French manner: '*Franquefore*'. With his dark eyes and thick black brows, he was often mistaken for a Berber or a Turk. He only had to open his mouth, however, for his interlocutors to abandon the East and let their minds rove over the whole of Northern Europe: "Danish?", "Swedish?", "Dutch?" Karl learned to let their doubts remain. He had already noticed that you only had to act in an elegant and refined manner, and no-one would believe that you came from the other side of the Rhine.

Karl endlessly watched Raimu and Renée Saint-Cyr in *L'École des Cocottes*: a 1935 film in which a young seamstress from Montmartre falls under the thumb of a teacher of etiquette, who wants to turn her into a socialite. "I'm certainly going to get a leg up into the upper class," the seamstress says, falsely innocent in a little black dress with a lace collar. Karl was enchanted by the vulgar turns of phrase that her mentor had to correct.

The Germans call the quick repartee that is so difficult to master in a language not one's own '*Witz*'. Karl set himself a challenge and, in a few years, could make jokes in French, had mastered wordplay and puns, and excelled at witticisms and double entendre.

When he was a teenager, he had discovered in his family library the works of Victor Hugo and Alexandre Dumas, and read them in French. After that he dug into Proust and Colette, read poetry and historical biography, and discovered the book that became his bible: the *Lettres de la princesse Palatine*. This princess was the sister-in-law of Louis XIV, who came from Heidelberg – "My compatriot," Karl would joke. Well before the Élysée treaty – de Gaulle and Adenauers' brotherly embrace – Karl had set up his own personal Franco-German reconciliation. "To be more French than the French, you have to be a foreigner," he realised. "This is not about patriotism: it is purely aesthetic."

On his first forays into Paris, young Lagerfeld inhaled the scents and sounds of the Latin Quarter. From there, he surveyed fashionable locations, discovering large private residences and museums. He greedily partook of the capital's private codes and snobberies. Amusing, cultivated and elegant, he walked among the Parisians – who themselves had not yet been able to resume the normal course of their lives, often living in apartments without indoor sanitation.

Thanks to his father, young Lagerfeld could meet his own needs from the best suppliers. At the age of twenty, he wore made-to-measure shirts from Hilditch & Key and fine suits made by Cifonelli, and begged his father to buy him a fine dark blue wool coat from a boutique opposite the Hôtel George V, where his father always stayed. Fashion provides elegant covers for what it wants to hide. Karl had already begun to create the philosophy that was to dominate his life: "I remember absolutely nothing. My thing is to burn my boats and to start again from zero."

Although he lived in Paris, Karl saw his first fashion show in Germany, on 13 December 1949. Elisabeth had picked up her social life again; she took her son to the Hotel Esplanade in Hamburg, where they used to stay in the days before they bought their house in the suburbs, on the high ground above the town. Christian Dior had come to Hamburg to display his latest collection to the burgeoning bourgeoisie of the new Federal Republic of Germany; and to the last British officers, who were just moving out of the Occupied Zone.

What better way to escape tragedy than through fashion, beauty, futility? The house of Dior had emerged three years earlier, financed by Marcel Boussac. Even in ruined Hamburg people had seen the designs for Dior's Corolle Collection, the 'New Look'. Did the Germans at the catwalk show know that, in 1944, Catherine, the couturier's younger sister, was deported to Ravensbrück for aiding the Resistance? Dior never mentioned it to the press. He only pleaded for "the return to the becoming, beautiful clothes of which women have been deprived for years."

The look that he proposed was sublime and revolutionary: nipped-in waist; high, round breasts; straight shoulders; legs bare from mid-calf. Karl vividly remembered being dazzled by this show of sheath dresses and mink muffs. Now that he lived in Paris, he wanted to re-create this magic, which had lodged itself so firmly in his war-child mentality: a beautiful dress is enough to clothe all manner of sorrows.

3

After less than two years in Paris, Karl Lagerfeld had penetrated the glittering heart of French pride: fashion. Though he was no longer the small boy who used to draw at the back of the class, he had not abandoned his passion. All day long he drew caricatures, sketched silhouettes and dressed paper figures, with the idea of becoming an illustrator. He hoarded plain exercise books and magazines full of inspiring images to cut out. Otto Lagerfeld financed him to begin with, but after the winter of 1954, Karl could earn his own living.

Six months earlier, he had taken part in a contest organised by Woolmark and the fashion arm of the Paris chamber of commerce: the 'Goncourt Prize' of couture. The winners would receive 300,000 francs each: six times the generous monthly allowance from his father. "I sent some drawings and then almost forgot about it – until a telegram arrived six months later…" So Karl claimed. In reality, this competition was an opportunity he intended to seize.

In a photograph taken on 25 November 1954, the three prize winners pose beside three models. On the right: Colette Bracchi, a young woman who won first prize in the tailoring section. She wears sandals in mid-winter and sports a pony tail, but seems full of confidence as she stands beside a model dressed in a black and white suit, below a little cap with a veil. Bracchi could not have guessed that, of the three winners, she was the one who would sink without trace, eclipsed by the other contestants' skill.

On the left, Karl's slightly anxious brown eyes can be spotted, his brown hair cut like James Dean. His design is by his side: a Cheviot coat in daffodil yellow for which he won, at the age of twenty-one, the first prize. As he says, "I had to do the sketch again in front of an official, to convince the jury that it was really done by me." With a hem reaching below the knees and buttons down the front, the overcoat was almost a classic – apart from its bright yellow colouration. The daring touch was its very low back, which gave the garment a sexy, modern look.

Seven sketches were chosen from the six thousand sent in from all over France. The jury, mainly composed of the couturiers Pierre Balmain, Jacques Fath and Hubert de Givenchy, kept back three drawings by the second young man, who seems to be hiding in the picture, though he is in the middle of the group. Yves Mathieu-Saint-Laurent looks incredibly thin in his dark suit; his huge spectacles almost conceal his skinny face. "The look of a young curate," they would later say in the Dior workrooms, when they saw him arrive. The jury, struck by the creativity of this eighteen-year-old, awarded him both first and third prize for his cocktail dress: a sinuous black sheath which left one shoulder bare.

The previous year, when the contest had just begun, this same boy won third prize. Christian Dior was one of the jurors. 'Monsieur Mathieu-Saint-Laurent' had already made his mark, in spite of his youth. The journalist Janie Samet, who was writing one of her first pieces for *L'Écho d'Oran*, had conducted a long interview with Mathieu-Saint-Laurent (who, like her, came from French Algeria). She remarked on his shyness and reported the following dictum, which had been enunciated in a strange, slightly hesitant voice: "Elegance: elegance means a dress that is too dazzling ever to be worn twice."

It was a twist of fate: Saint Laurent and Lagerfeld, singled out at the same time. One hailed from the light-filled shores of the Mediterranean, the other from the dark riverbanks of the Elbe. Karl was quick to notice Yves' talent – who appreciated the elegance of a pencil sketch, the distinction of a line, the intelligence of a cut more than him? For his part, Yves loved Karl's humour, his ease and his organisational skills. Yves enjoyed many spins in the Mercedes coupé that Otto gave his son after his success in the competition. Later, when their rivalry achieved legendary heights, their fashion clans pretended to forget that Yves and Lagerfeld had ever been friends. For the time being, however, they were often seen together at the Bar des Théâtres – or on Avenue Montaigne, where they worked more or less opposite one another, Yves for Dior and Karl for Balmain, a couple of streets away from Rue François-Ier.

Balmain recruited Lagerfeld as an assistant. He was tasked (along with four others) with 'spicing up' the couturier's designs. "Horrible!" Lagerfeld still remembered, sixty years later. "Dreadful working conditions for miserable pay. The high fashion of the time was humiliation and spite!" Balmain asked his young apprentice to design the Florilège collection – "Clothes for the shop, aimed at bourgeoise housewives, short jackets over skirts."

Saint Laurent had more luck at Dior. This was the great couture house of the moment, the most inventive and the most desirable. Karl knew it – he still recalled his amazement at that first fashion show at the Hotel Esplanade in Hamburg. At any rate, Yves had been a star among the pupils of the Paris Chamber of Commerce fashion school. He served his apprenticeship at the same time as Karl, although they had different classes and teachers.

These two young men, so alike and yet so different, were soon to disrupt the fashion scene and the aesthetic of their time. Spoilt children, both gay, and both – Saint Laurent and Lagerfeld – able to count on their families' support. "Send the bill to my father" – how often did each say that: Yves at the fabric shops, from which he dressed his sister; Karl at Hilditch & Key, where Otto gave him open credit? Charles Mathieu-Saint-Laurent had taken it upon himself to present his son to one of his friends,

Michel de Brunhoff, the editor-in-chief of French *Vogue*. De Brunhoff, struck by the young man's talent, had shown his drawings to Christian Dior, who engaged him in 1955.

Lucienne Mathieu-Saint-Laurent accompanied her son everywhere. She was charming: one of those elegant women whose dressmaker came weekly to her house in Oran, with fabrics and patterns copied from the Paris fashion houses. A very warm woman, she was sometimes demonstrative to excess. "Stop doing your Pied-Noir bit!" Yves used to grumble at her, when she exaggerated her anger or admiration.

Karl saw her as the diametric opposite to his own mother. Mrs Lagerfeld specialised in irony, both in her expression and with her words. To sustain the comparison with the warm-hearted Lucienne, Karl took to inventing a number of entertaining witticisms for Elisabeth, as well as an elegant past. He claimed that before the war, she used to come to Paris to buy her clothes from Madeleine Vionnet. He did not push his luck, however, by presenting her to his friends or to the world of fashion – unlike Yves, who introduced his mother to Monsieur Dior.

Lucienne and Elisabeth had a number of features in common. The first was that they had protected their sons since childhood after they realised they were gay. Mrs Lagerfeld chose reassuring denial. Yves' mother brushed off any suspicions that her son was, as it was said back then, 'a pansy'. "No, you see," she said to Yves' sister Brigitte. "He is like the angels; in other words he has no sexuality." In Oran, the other boys drowned the young Mathieu-Saint-Laurent in sarcastic comments, while in the countryside of Schleswig-Holstein, young Lagerfeld learned to distinguish himself from the other children, whom he regarded with disdain. Both experienced the solitude engendered by difference. Their mothers were smothering; each in her own way turned her boy into a little king.

When they joined Dior and Balmain, Saint Laurent and Lagerfeld marked their entrance into the world of work, money, success, and in some ways, romance. Their ambitions differed slightly, nevertheless. Yves wanted to create outstanding dresses, the dresses that dreams were made of. Lagerfeld, in contrast, accepted that 'fashion is superficial'. He liked adapting to any constraints, working quickly and tirelessly, and with a strong sense of what was not yet then called 'marketing'. He knew that working for Balmain was infinitely less prestigious than designing for Dior – but "I wanted to serve my apprenticeship," he later claimed.

Yves seemed sometimes to be creeping along the walls. He spoke in a whisper, never deviating from his shyness, except in the company of close friends. "He is funny, batty, skinny, agile and has a very pointed nose," Lagerfeld said admiringly, at the time; he often made sketches of his friend, adding speech bubbles filled with jokes.

"Karl has a romantic face, dark eyes, and full, well-defined lips, which gave him a sulky look above a square, determined chin" – this is how Victoire Doutreleau

(Dior's top model, whose favours were vied for by both Saint Laurent and Lagerfeld) described him. It is true that Lagerfeld was attractive in a very individual way. Yves and Victoire loved it when their friend re-created 'Monsieur Balmain' for them – a chubby, bald man with a small moustache and snobbish airs. "Imagine – his mother came to the workshop one day and said: 'If I learn that my son is homosexual, I shall kill him!' And an aged Russian princess who was waiting for a fitting shouted: 'Fire!'" They laughed uproariously when they were with Lagerfeld, and it was not unheard of for the three friends, after hours spent drinking and smoking (except for Karl, who touched neither alcohol nor cigarettes), to fall asleep on the drawing room carpet at 31 Rue de Tournon, the apartment Karl had moved to after he found his first job. Katherine Mansfield lived in the same building, and Karl read her poetry and novels. In the morning, the young German would drop Yves and Victoire off at Dior in his cream-coloured convertible.

Yves had bought himself a large studio on the ground floor of a building in Square Pétrarque, in the sixteenth arrondissement – his green velvet sofa-bed resided in a blue velvet alcove. The three friends began again every evening, meeting either at Karl's flat, or at Yves'. Then they would go out. Saint Laurent enjoyed sentimental entanglements and intrigue, and went clubbing in the more sordid areas of Paris. Karl was somewhat scornful about herds of young women; he much preferred listening to the latest Miles

Davis or the motets of Anton Bruckner to visiting the bars where Saint Laurent played at intimidating the bad boys. "I have nothing to prove and their propositioning annoys me," he said disdainfully about Le Fiacre, the little club on the Rue du Cherche-Midi where men danced the Charleston together. "There are too many queens." As he nauseously stared down into the black hole of a gay club where Yves would succumb to the first light contact, Karl would amuse his friends by saying "No thank you; I have everything I need and I don't use it."

Frequent moments of intense rivalry flared between Yves and Karl. Victoire, a ravishing and entertaining brunette, used to exploit this. One day, Karl gave her a bundle of sketches in which she appeared in outfits that retraced the history of fashion, from the 1890s to the street urchin style of the day. The following day, Yves dedicated a sketch of a sheath evening dress to her: "To the girl who wears my dresses so beautifully." Their circle, soon joined by Anne-Marie Poupard (later to become Anne-Marie Muñoz), developed in a gloriously light-hearted way, with weekends in Deauville and dinners at the Closerie des Lilas.

In autumn 1957, an event occurred that deepened the gulf between the two friends. Christian Dior had gone to take another of his frequent slimming holidays at Montecatini, the thermal resort in Tuscany, when he suddenly died of a heart attack. As the most prominent couturier of the day, his unexpected death sent shock waves throughout France. The second shock wave followed soon after: the fashion house promoted young Yves to the board of directors.

That a young man of only twenty-one should take over from 'Monsieur Dior' was an important event, as well as a consecration. It was a time of intense anxiety and violent creativity for Saint Laurent, who decided to dispense with 'Mathieu' and shorten his signature. His burgeoning glory eclipsed Karl, who had yet to invent anything – and it also made Yves far less available.

One evening, the correspondent of *Harper's Bazaar* invited Yves to dine with a prominent young couple, the painter Bernard Buffet and his companion Pierre Bergé. Yves was an admirer of Buffet's paintings, but that evening he was dazzled by his mentor's erudition and sense of humour. Bergé, a twenty-seven-year-old, had made Buffet's work universally desirable. "A strange young man, shy, always squeezed into very tight jackets as if he wanted to protect himself from the world," – this was Bergé's first impression of Saint Laurent. He later wrote: "Yves made me think of a seminarian, very serious and very timid."

Saint Laurent's talent (or genius) was not in any doubt. Henceforward, he could also rely on a partner who possessed plenty of that quality which was totally absent from his nature: business sense. With Bergé, his Pygmalion lover, he established his own house, presenting the first haute couture collection under his name in 1962. Little by little, he grew apart from his former friends. Bergé always seemed jealous of Yves' complicity with Victoire, of his gales of laughter at Karl's jokes. The group continued to meet occasionally, here and there, but Yves had become familiar with fame while Karl, after a stint with Patou, was still working for others.

Lagerfeld and Bergé understood each other. Were they not more cultivated and more enterprising than everyone around them? But Bergé was serious and proud, often arrogant. He proclaimed the genius of Saint Laurent on all sides, barely bothering to conceal his disdain for other designers. Each time a possible rivalry between Yves and Karl was mentioned, Bergé brushed it aside, suggesting that "They are just not in the same league."

When her son went to work with Balmain, Elisabeth Lagerfeld said, with characteristically brutal frankness, "So, you are just going to be a retailer." Balmain would later pretend to laugh at couturiers who considered themselves artists. Still, Lagerfeld was better than anyone at assessing the elegance of a dress, the audacity of a dinner jacket, the seductive quality of the safari suits Saint Laurent re-invented. He kept a design for a theatrical costume signed *YSL* on his mantelpiece for years. The fluidity of a skirt, the set of a collar – he understood every technical difficulty, and knew how ideas could be born at the drawing table. Karl knew he was more cultivated and more disciplined than Saint Laurent – he just lacked the neurotic genius of his friend.

"I wasn't jealous," he was to say at a much later date. Was this because he believed he would make his own destiny? One day, Yves and Bergé went with him to visit

"Madame Zirakian, a fortune-teller in a basement in Rue de Maubeuge." Did the other two men listen to what she told them? "She said to Yves: 'It's all good now but it will end quite quickly.' And to me: 'It will begin for you when it ends for the others.'"

Otto Lagerfeld died on 4 July 1967, at the age of eighty-seven. He had retired ten years previously, leaving Hamburg and the mists of the Elbe for Baden-Baden, the fashionable spa resort in the Black Forest.

Was Karl affected by his death? He still spoke of his father with disdain: "He always wore a hat, carried a cane and wore suits of pale grey salt and pepper tweed, which I hate. He was not like me at all." This was all he had to say. He barely mentioned his father's death to his friends that year.

From then on, he gradually effaced his father's memory, as one erases details from a drawing. He often ascribed new origins to him, sometimes aristocratic ones: "My father was Swedish, he was a baron," he claimed in some of his early interviews. That saved him from having to answer questions about Otto's industrial past during the war. When, years later, Elisabeth Lagerfeld died, Karl re-invented his arrival in Paris in 1952, "at the age of fourteen," accompanied by his mother alone. This killed two birds with one stone: he shaved five years off his age and re-invented a couple – without Otto.

He claimed that Elisabeth only told him about his father's death three weeks after it happened, adding: "Anyway, you don't like funerals." This relegated Otto's passing to the status of an anecdote: the ultimate tweak to his Oedipal dream.

4

Behind the wheel of a stylish car (after the Mercedes his father gave him, he bought himself a Bentley) Karl Lagerfeld could pass for a well-heeled playboy – which, truth be told, he was. Though people assumed him to be the heir to a rich family of industrialists, he soon began to earn a good living.

He became the artistic director of Patou in 1959, but found himself bored stiff designing two annual collections, each with about sixty new designs. 'Monsieur Gabriel', the spitting image of the French actor Raimu, ruled the workshop, and 'Madame Alphonsine' was the star of the head seamstresses. Eternally dressed in a grey pullover and flannel skirt, armed with her box of pins, Madame Alphonsine was unrivalled in her ability to build up *toiles*; she ruled her workforce with an iron rod. If a dress fell well, she would always reiterate the same vulgar phrase: "It falls like a turd from the sixth floor." Karl began to imitate her, repeating the magic phrase in his Hamburg accent. It was here that he at last learned his trade.

By now, Lagerfeld could produce a perfect fashion drawing, with notes of all the technical details, in a matter of minutes. His geographical sketch-maps showed the reef of the pleats, the flaps and the yokes – what other designer developed such an eye for detail?

At this time, he was designing for a series of labels. He was the first person to work freelance in this manner and it gave him a considerable income. After Rue de Tournon, he set his heart on 7 Quai Voltaire. This fine block of flats had plenty of history. It was said to have been here that the seductive pianist Misia Sert used to meet Coco Chanel. The Marquis de Cuevas, the Chilean choreographer, lived on the ground floor and dancers from the *corps de ballet* went in and out all day. Upstairs lived the young Colombe Pringle, daughter of the novelist Flore Groult and a future journalist; she used to admire Lagerfeld's Bentley when it was parked in the paved courtyard.

Meanwhile, Yves and Pierre Bergé wanted to make Saint Laurent an exclusive brand. Karl, in contrast, designed shoes for Charles Jourdan, bags for the Italian Krizia, coats for Max Mara, sunglasses and even underwear for a dozen or so other labels. Why did he not try to create under his own name? "This is an old feeling that came with me from Hamburg," he told me. "In Hamburg, unlike in Oran, nothing is less elegant than having your name over the door. You can be an industrialist, a banker but not a shopkeeper." *A shopkeeper…* Pierre Bergé must have appreciated that.

With his keen sense for fashion, Lagerfeld soon realised that haute couture was on the decline, in spite of all the dedicated professionals who hung onto it like a mantra.

Pierre Cardin, who opened his boutique Homme in 1957, and two years later presented a ready-to-wear collection, was suspended from the fashion chamber of commerce for five years. Nevertheless, his success did not falter. The youth of the day fought over the mini skirt, invented by the British designer, Mary Quant. Little jersey dresses designed by Courrèges were in all the magazines. Even rich clients wanted something more light-hearted, an outfit bought on a whim rather than after three fittings.

It was brave nevertheless, for a young man like Karl, trained in haute couture, to take off in the direction of prêt-à-porter. But he was after money, rapid success and the sense of embodying his age.

He undertook a new venture in 1963, offering his designs to Gabrielle Aghion, who had launched Chloé, the first up-market prêt-à-porter label, with her business partner Jacques Lenoir. A small, rotund brunette, 'Gaby' Aghion belonged to a liberal middle-class Egyptian family of Francophiles; she had dreamed up her first gowns at home, twelve years previously. An amusing, energetic woman, she had enough knowledge of French society to know what elegant ladies desired, combined with the sense to direct a business. The press supported her from the start, especially the founding editor of *Elle*, Hélène Lazareff, and in 1956, her first collection was presented at the Café de Flore, to plaudits from various magazines.

After this success, she set up a small workshop with about a dozen employees, using stylists who worked exclusively for her label. Under normal circumstances, she should have turned her back on Lagerfeld, this multi-brand mercenary who snobbishly expressed his distaste when she consorted – alongside her Communist husband Raymond Aghion – with the cream of the Party. Lagerfeld, however, seduced her with his inventive sketches, in particular a beige shantung dress worn with yellow tights. His conversation was so entertaining, so erudite, that it enchanted Gabrielle, this friend of the poets Éluard and Aragon. "Of all the stylists I have ever worked with, Karl was the only real intellectual," she remarked.

Lagerfeld often called himself 'Roland Karl'. Now, however, he abandoned this French surname and blossomed. Though his short first name was so very German, it was easy to pronounce in any language.

Gaby was an intelligent and delightful woman. In the afternoon, when they were working together at the large table in the studio, or in the evening, when they were driven home together in Gabrielle's car, their ideas seemed to harmonise. At first, Gabrielle turned her nose up at Karl's proposals: "Too many frills, too many superfluous effects. You need to lighten up," she would say. But Lagerfeld was quick to learn, and demonstrated an inventiveness and productivity hitherto unheard of in her workroom. "My mother got on very well with him," reports Gabrielle's son, Philippe Aghion, now teaching economics at the Collège de France. "Karl brought his ideas and his creativity, and she sorted through his sketches, persuading him to cut back and minimalize. In short, to suppress his tendency to go 'over the top' which, behind his back, she used to call 'his German side'."

Theirs was a great partnership, and in 1966, Gaby handed over the direction of design. At thirty-three, Karl made a masterly job of designing long skirts, floating blouses and loose-fitting dresses that hardly seemed to touch the body. The work force in the studio adored him: a designer who sketched clothes with such precision that they knew immediately where to place the waist on a jacket or the sleeve on a kimono. "You would think he had spent his life in a couture studio," said Anita Briey, a young seamstress from Burgundy who had come to work for Chloé after starting with Chanel.

The models were allowed to choose what they would wear at the fashion shows. Balmain or Patou always maintained a formal atmosphere, and their clientele seemed to be about one hundred and twenty years old – Chloé's fashion was delightfully light and witty in comparison. No-one talked of elegance anymore; the word was weighed down by protocol. When the term 'chic' emerged, fashion started to fizz. Chloé's turnover took off. "The Karl effect," as journalists were starting to say.

Despite this, his reputation had not spread beyond the circle of those who knew him. All over Paris, other designers were beginning to flourish. Sonia Rykiel established her own company under her own name in 1965, focusing on emancipated women, after launching a collection of little pullovers which caught the eye of Audrey Hepburn. One year earlier, Elie and Jacqueline

Jacobson captivated young people with the creation of Dorothée Bis. "Haute couture is dead," Emmanuelle Kahn was to claim; her oversized spectacles appeared on the noses of Catherine Deneuve and David Bowie. "I want to design for the street. A kind of socialist fashion for the masses."

Karl Lagerfeld might have followed the same route, becoming a 'creator' who sold his clothes under his own name. What twist did he want to give to his career? "I had no ambition," he claimed. A polyglot like his father, he went to work in Japan and Italy. It was in Rome that he heard about the Fendi sisters, who were looking for a designer for their furs. Adele Fendi, a Roman matriarch, still reigned their shop in Via Piave, which was presided over by a photograph of her five daughters in their wedding dresses. The sisters were seduced by Karl. He set himself up in Piazza di Spagna for several weeks of the year, in one of the suites of Hotel Hassler; he liked its Pompeian ochre paint and its proximity to Palazzo Fendi.

To escape their mother's influence, the five sisters moved their salon to a former cinema in Via Frattina – "half Visconti film, half brothel," was Karl's comment. He always arrived with an armful of designs. Once there, he would produce other designs: long pelisses with yokes which looked like capes, or neat blousons in leather and sable, which the models would wear over pony-skin jodhpurs. He modernised the 'look' of the Roman matrons, taking scissors to their heavy mink coats – he even designed their logo one day. This was one of his selling points: he produced a lot of designs very quickly, and his clothes would always sell.

If he wanted to, he could have enjoyed a dazzling career abroad. However, this would mean an end to his competition with Saint Laurent, and it was to continue this rivalry that he remained in France. In Paris, 1966, Prince Yves also turned to prêt-à-porter, reigning over the new fashion codes – and a small band of admirers. Success had changed this shy, nervous young man. He spent every evening surrounded by a half dozen good-looking, slightly decadent young adults who came to Place Vauban, where he had set up house with Bergé, to drink alcohol and get high on Moroccan kif. The willowy silhouette of Betty Catroux could be seen dancing in the shadows, while Loulou de la Falaise giggled in the kitchen; the first did not work, except to inspire people, while the second never stopped designing accessories to complement the dinner jackets and transparent blouses that made the Saint Laurent woman a canny mixture of power and sex.

Pierre Bergé was fascinated by the aristocracy: those French families whose names included a 'noble particle' (de, d' or du), whose roots were entrenched in the France of the past, and who were still entertaining people in their castles and private residences. It was not unusual for Yves and him to dine at the house of a Baroness, who would make it a point of honour to wear her Saint Laurent suit; the couple often ended the evening in the gay clubs that were opening across Paris. To be accepted by the amazingly exclusive Saint Laurent clan had become the dream of all the playboys in the capital. Needless to say, when the strikes and demonstrations of May 1968 occurred, they hardly touched Saint Laurent's group, who were already at ease with sexual liberation and Dadaist slogans.

Karl Lagerfeld may have bought himself a Rolls-Royce, but he was still more accessible than Saint Laurent and less elitist. Bit by bit, he began body building in a gym in Rue Sainte-Anne, where all the gigolos did their training. At the Piscine Deligny swimming pool, his superb body, finely tuned by exercise and encased in a tight 1930s swimming costume, caused a sensation when he paraded along the decking in high-heeled mules. Karl was easily mistaken for the eccentric son of German aristocrats – or Swedish, or even Danish, thanks to the mysterious aura with which he surrounded his father – because he always told stories about life in the *châteaux,* and generously paid for dinners at Brasserie Lipp. In actual fact, this 'milk rich' young man (as those who thought he was the direct heir to the Nestlé milk fortune used to call him) worked like a demon.

He had a gang of his own, too. 'Karl's group' (as they were known, to distinguish them from the 'Saint Laurent clan') was more international; they spoke English, the language that Yves had to have translated for him by Loulou de la Falaise. Sexy black moustaches, gold rings in the ear and Mexican boots: Antonio Lopez and Juan Ramos had been the pillars of the group since their arrival in Paris in 1969. Lopez was a talented illustrator, Ramos his art director and former lover. It can be said without exaggeration that Karl was exceedingly attracted to these two Puerto Ricans when they arrived in Paris. "It was like a breath of fresh air from America arriving in this hidebound, provincial place," he said.

They were amusing, creative and obsessively keen hunters of beauty. "Antonio wanted everything to be beautiful," Karl commented. "Sometimes too beautiful. In his drawings, he refused to include the models' imperfections." Despite this, Karl saw at once what he could learn from the designer, whose genius he sincerely admired. Juan and Antonio seemed considerably more evolved than the people of old Europe. They were cultured, but had liberated themselves from rules. Lopez was immensely knowledgeable about the history of art and extraordinarily successful at combining the colour values of fifteenth-century Florence – oranges and pistachio greens, juxtapositions of the warm and the cool – with the sexiest, most garish colour schemes of the Harlem gay scene. He worked in advertising, in fashion, for magazines and for himself, with a total disregard for convention.

Almost every morning, Juan took Karl to a bookshop, La Hune, a couple of paces from the Café de Flore. Photographs, paintings, architectural drawings, strip cartoons, essays signed by young illustrators from New York with whom he had worked – Juan scooped it all up. Ramos would then cut up the pages to make collages, introducing Karl to this wonderful plundering of the centuries and continents that fed his imagination. With them at his side, Karl did not only dream up dresses; he built a global aesthetic. He had always read a lot – now he was completing his visual library. In fact, he learned to become much more than a dress designer: he became the inventor of what was later to be called, more prosaically, 'the universe of a brand'.

New faces from the United States followed in Antonio and Juan's wake. Corey Tippin came first, a gorgeous apprentice model, eighteen years old with peroxided hair, always on the lookout for adventure and amusement. Then came Pat Cleveland, the first mixed-race model to hit the catwalk, and a beautiful young woman with remarkable teeth, Donna Jordan, who attracted attention by swaying along on impossibly high heels.

This little gang thought they had arrived in the City of Light, but instead found Paris drab, dirty and gloomy. "We thought we were climbing the heights of beauty and eccentricity, but it was the reverse," said Corey Tippin recently. "Pop culture had not yet crossed the Atlantic and the city was lacklustre and stodgy." In New York, black people and Puerto Ricans were beginning to shake up the traditional white American culture. In France, the uprisings of May '68 had done away with the shackles of bourgeois convention, but as of yet society took no notice of minorities, diversity, or those in search of alternative culture. The Americans were left speechless at their first catwalk show in Paris, the fashion capital of the world: the models from the haute couture houses paraded in silence, holding a little card bearing the number of their outfit. It was as if rock and roll and the winds of change had yet to blow through the catwalk. "Glamour" – that word so often repeated by Pat and Donna – was not yet common parlance on the banks of the Seine.

After that, Lagerfeld viewed his adoptive city through their eyes, and hoped for better things. He had described them as "a breath of fresh air" from the "provincial" – this being the greatest dread of a man who had changed country to open his frontiers.

That evening, as they dined together in Saint-Germain-des-Prés, the seductive breeze of modern life danced around their table. "Juan was the most demonstrative, Antonio the most creative," noted Florentine Pabst, a Hamburg journalist who met them during the 1970s, "but Karl remained at the centre because he was the most intelligent." Florentine had heard about Lagerfeld a few years earlier, when she discovered the collection he had designed for Charles Jourdan. She was struck by his level of culture, and by this sophisticated, literary German who towered over everyone else's heads. She could not imagine a group of people existing who were more inventive, more bohemian than those who swarmed around Karl: "They regarded themselves as artists in the best sense of the word. They did things with a kind of innocence and engagement, without motivation. [...] Gratuitously."

They were known as 'Karl's group', and in fact were generously supported by him. For Antonio and Juan, he rented a studio in Rue Bonaparte, and later an apartment in Boulevard Saint-Germain, paid restaurant bills, handed out shirts, dresses and expensive presents. Corey signed on with various model agencies, but she was chasing after work until Antonio suggested she become a make-up artist. Pat Cleveland and Donna Jordan took photographs, but blew the money on vintage dresses and evenings out. "Karl became our sponsor," Corey recalled.

Karl moved house again, this time into an enormous apartment on the first floor of a town house, 35 Rue de l'Université. He furnished it entirely with objects from Dunand and valuable lacquer pieces. This is where he threw fabulous dinner parties to amaze his American friends.

In summer, he invited the little group to a house he had rented in Saint-Tropez. Antonio and Juan were highly amused to see their friend showing off his muscles by the swimming pool, but withdrawing prudishly at the first sign of flirting. The boys were eager to involve themselves in any suggestion of cruising, and Corey, who had been a go-go dancer in New York, would sway provocatively by the table reserved by Karl in the fashionable local clubs. But despite this, Lagerfeld always seemed more of a voyeur than an actor. He was entertained by his circle of henchmen, preferring them to a harem of lovers. And still, he had not attained the aura he aspired to – the personal distinction, the confirmation that he was the best student of his era.

After Otto's death, Karl brought Elisabeth Lagerfeld to live with him in Paris, in a room at the end of his apartment. A son living with his seventy-three-year-old mother caused quite a stir. The New York group never knew quite what to do when she appeared at tea-time, dressed by her son in a pair of flowing trousers and a silk blouse of his design. She had the same eyes as Karl, framed by white hair, and almost the same accent when she spoke French. Antonio drew her portrait more than once, reclining on her sofa reading German newspapers.

In summer, Corey and Juan would go on the train to Saint-Tropez with 'Mutti' (as they called her for a joke); that meant sitting opposite this friendly, albeit stiff woman – always portrayed by her son as the statue of the Commendatore in Mozart's Don Giovanni.

Madame Lagerfeld had a sense of propriety, in contrast with the Americans, who obeyed no rules. The last time they made the journey to the Côte d'Azur together, Corey was captivated to see the way Mutti slipped her son money under the table in the restaurant car, so that he could pay for lunch.

Lagerfeld's habits, his erudition, his money and his mother – all of these traits added up to a legend. Elisabeth was alleged to keep an eye on him, and he always returned early in the evening to please her. He was thought to have inherited his discipline from her educational methods – but in fact they made a very equal couple. Antonio, Juan and Corey knew that Andy would love her.

5

It was October 1970, and Andy Warhol was coming to Paris. The New York group were feverish with excitement when they heard. Antonio, Juan, Corey and Donna belonged to the hip generation – while in America, all of them were regular visitors to The Factory: the studio in the heart of Manhattan, at 33 Union Square, where the master of Pop Art made his silk-screen prints. They knew what a sensation Warhol would cause in France. With his silver wig (very obviously synthetic, from a distance of ten metres), his peroxided eyebrows and the little tape recorder in the pocket of his blazer, the star of the underground always heralded a frenzy of parties and events.

Even so, Warhol was quite a disconcerting figure. He spoke little, punctuating other people's conversation with the word 'Gee', uttered in a small, high voice. Surrounded by crowds of handsome young admirers, he walked stiffly and observed them all with myopic eyes. Two years beforehand, a militant feminist had emptied her revolver into him outside the entrance to The Factory. Since then, he had been forced to wear a medical corset. "I've got more stitches in me than a Dior dress," he declared, deadpan, when he arrived at Orly Airport.

The Parisian world of fashion and art found Warhol amazingly smart and subversive. His kitsch appearance caused a sensation amongst all the dinner jackets during the party Marie-Hélène de Rothschild threw in his honour. For a number of years, his *Campbell's Soup Cans* and prints of film stars such as Marilyn Monroe had placed him at the forefront of the artistic avant-garde. He had not quite attained the apotheosis he was to reach later in the world of contemporary art, but his aphorisms already riveted the journalists. Carefully prepared in the wings, they earned him the reputation of a man with a profound and incisive mind. If you knew 'Andy', you could be sure that all the elite circles would welcome you. And, as 'Karl's group' discovered, they were well placed to join him.

The artist had come to Paris to make a feature film, *L'Amour*, with a screenplay by himself and Paul Morrissey, a New York Irishman who had become a figure in underground cinema. Warhol's first films were often experimental, repeating a single motif the way his paintings did; in *Sleep*, the American poet John Giorno is seen sleeping for five hours and twenty-one minutes.

This time he promised a story: two girls from rural America arrive in Paris in search of a rich husband. *Gold Diggers 71* was the code name of the script. All the bolder beauties of the fashion world were hoping for a small part in it. The filming took place at Le Sept, the smartest location of the day, located at 7 Rue Saint-Anne.

It was a glamorous restaurant known vengefully by those not admitted as 'Maxim's for queens'. Every evening, it buzzed with models and intellectuals, including the semiologist Roland Barthes and Michel Guy, later to be appointed Minister of Culture in Valéry Giscard d'Estaing's government.

Fabrice Emaer, the proprietor of the club, greeted his clients every evening with the words *'Bonjour, bébé d'amour'* ('Hi, love child'). He was thrilled to host Warhol. Two years earlier, he, like the American artist, had been wounded – by a gangster who shot him one Saturday night and stole the club's takings. This shared trauma resulted in an electrifying atmosphere of danger, which hovered over *L'Amour*.

The New York group knew that this was their opportunity to shine. "As soon as he saw him, Andy wanted Karl in his film," Corey Tippin remembered. "I think he liked everything. Karl's sexy side, his culture, but also his kitsch and his wit." Corey had been given a small role in the film, and he organised the encounter.

Warhol had never heard of Karl Lagerfeld in the United States. Yves Saint Laurent – yes, he knew him. Several years earlier, the New York press had dubbed him 'King of Fashion'. The elegance of his dresses; the audacity of the dinner jackets worn by Catherine Deneuve, the most famous French film star abroad; and the seductive quality of his safari suits had won him success world-wide. At the age of thirty-seven, Karl had revolutionised nothing.

Nevertheless, when Juan and Corey, beside themselves with excitement, informed Lagerfeld that Warhol was looking for locations to film, Lagerfeld suggested that some of the scenes could be filmed in his apartment, 35 Rue de l'Université. A lacquer table by Dunand, furniture by Fontana and some Lalannes – Warhol immediately loved his Art Deco furnishings. Andrée Putman, whom Karl met in 1968, had advised Karl on his décor. At the time, Putman was a lowly stylist, working first for Prisunic and then for the Mafia agency, but she had married the collector, publisher and art critic Jacques Putman, and was familiar with artists such as Pierre Alechinsky, Bram van Velde, Alberto Giacometti and Niki de Saint Phalle. A large, stately blonde, Putman had an unrivalled talent for finding talented decorators or buying furnishings and works of art in the auction houses of Paris and New York. Karl's collection took shape partly thanks to her, and he owed to her the finest rooms in his apartment.

The location was sumptuous, and Lagerfeld cannily made it more attractive by declaring it to be haunted: "This block of flats is under a curse." How could Warhol resist?

As expected, Warhol was very aware of Mrs Lagerfeld's presence. At the age of forty-two, he also lived with his mother, who dwelled in the basement of his house in Lexington Avenue. He felt a twinge of familiarity when he heard Elisabeth speaking English with that slight German accent; it sounded just like the Czech inflections of Julia Warhola. Julia never really learned to speak American English, although she emigrated to the States in 1921.

Andy adored his mother, and had lived in cosy intimacy with her since the death of his father when he was fourteen.

Of course, Julia did not have the elegance of Elisabeth Lagerfeld. She came from a far more working-class background, and her son was sometimes embarrassed by her country ways. But she had cared for him when he was a frail youngster, often bedbound, with exemplary unselfishness and love. Since then he had conducted a relationship with her that was based partly on deep affection, partly on utility. She fed his innumerable cats, cut out pictures from magazines for him and even made drawings for little books that they wrote together, which were signed by them both. "I'm a mother's boy," Warhol would often say.

Lagerfeld would never have used such an expression. Elisabeth remained far too Prussian to allow such a lack of constraint from her son. When the American artist was introduced to her, she immediately turned the conversation to New York and Paris, offered a cup of tea and hardly raised an eyebrow when the little gang prepared the apartment for the filming. Warhol, who liked nothing better than polite small talk, was very impressed. But it was Karl whom Andy was most drawn to. He found him "flamboyant, well-dressed and muscular" – so Corey Tippin told me.

Andy Warhol and Karl Lagerfeld: the media monster of the day and the man who would later become one. Warhol picked up his screenplay again and quickly added a role for Lagerfeld: a German aristocrat whom both girls try to seduce, while on their quest for a husband. These lady leads were Donna Jordan, the girl with the wonderful teeth who was always out on the razzle with Corey Tippin, and Jane Forth, a young diaphanous beauty with plucked-out eyebrows.

There were several unexpected similarities between the Prussian-French couturier and the American artist. They both loved art and film. Karl performed admirably in Warhol's territory; his conversation sparkled, and he could switch from a slightly off-colour joke to a detailed analysis of *Nosferatu*, Murnau's masterpiece (of which he possessed a copy) in perfect English. He alternated puns with literary quotations, and knew how to pull out all the stops to attract Warhol: this man from New York, who was currently the focus of Paris.

Around them, their little gang of amateur actors continued to party. Sex, drugs, rock 'n' roll: Corey and his group of friends flirted and got high every evening, slept until early afternoon, worked when they felt like it or when their money ran out. Andy and Karl kept well away from the amphetamines, which were served in bowls like sweets. "I don't like alcohol, I don't like drugs and I have never been obsessed with sex," Lagerfeld would say; he drank only Coca-Cola.

Warhol loved to be surrounded by good-looking boys, but he had a complex about his physique and the scars left by the many operations he had undergone since the attack. He was provocative, asking women crude questions about their husbands' genitals; when a young man appealed to him, on the other hand, he readily slipped into the role of a timid and amorous adolescent. As a voyeur, he preferred filming people – or, better yet, recording what they said with his little tape recorder, which never left him.

Lagerfeld was no more forward than Warhol. Still, he did not possess Warhol's neurotic weirdness: the way he outwardly eschewed social life while revelling in dinner parties, which he would later describe in his journal, in great detail. Lagerfeld did not conceal his anger when Andy, encouraged by Paul Morrissey, maliciously planned a sex scene between Karl and Patti D'Arbanville, the actress and model who had inspired her boyfriend Cat Stevens to name a song after her. From behind the camera, Warhol requested that the scene be re-filmed several times. "He has a reckless side that I lack," Lagerfeld joked. With the film long forgotten, their voracious kiss is the only record of that moment.

L'Amour was far from being a masterpiece. It was panned when it was released, except by the film critic of *Le Monde*, who compared it (far too) favourably to a film by Éric Rohmer. On the screen, the image jumps and wobbles, and the actors ham their way through it, but Karl comes out rather well. Wearing a silk shirt, white jeans and a broad belt, he shimmies his way naturally through the improbable story, as the models recruited by Warhol mumble their words. The press hardly mentioned him; he was unknown to the wider public.

It would have been impossible for Karl and the Americans to monopolise the high priest of Pop Art. Paris was alive with stories about the little gang, of their incomparable glamour and their provocative deeds.

Lagerfeld could not be the only one to benefit from the arrival of counter-culture in Europe. Saint Laurent was the prince of fashion, and would not be usurped – or at any rate, Pierre Bergé was not about to let it happen.

"One evening, Yves and Pierre gave a party in honour of Andy at their place," Corey Tippin remembers. It was one of those evenings to which the entire fashion world would have liked to have been invited; even Karl's friends would have killed for an invitation. A few years earlier, Corey and Donna Jordan had encountered Saint Laurent and his mentor at La Coupole in the Boulevard de Montparnasse. Karl was not there. As a result, they managed to get themselves invited to the party, disregarding this minor betrayal of the man who generously paid their bills.

Yves had not yet met Warhol. He assembled his whole clan in Place Vauban for the occasion. Helmut Berger was there, as handsome and decadent as he was in *The Damned* – Visconti's film, released the previous year, which had made a profound impression with its orgy of Nazi officers before the Night of the Long Knives. With his peroxided hair, Berger might have been expected (like his character) to rise again as the drag queen 'Marlene', in suspenders and a top hat, to sing in German, his mother tongue. For the time being, he chatted with Omar Sharif, the star of *Lawrence of Arabia* and *Doctor Zhivago*. One room had a television showing pornographic films. "There was an atmosphere of crazy excitement," said Corey, who was delighted to be among the elite of this exclusive coterie. Donna Jordan played the spoilt child, everyone ran after Yves' dog, the guests drank too much, Patti D'Arbanville got into a fight with Donna – in short, the evening was a resounding success. The crew of *L'Amour* all paraded around Saint Laurent. The only absentee was Karl Lagerfeld.

Warhol knew how to arouse desire. Every time he visited Paris, he stayed with the Comtesse Brandolini, sister-in-law of Gianni Agnelli, and allowed his manager, Fred Hughes, to sell their portraits to rich families. In the evenings, he went out. "As soon as he arrived at the door of a club, even if it was packed, space would be made for him and for his courtiers," said the photographer Philippe Morillon, who was soon to work with Warhol's entourage. "His presence alone was the proof of a successful evening." Pierre Bergé, who had Warhol to dinner several times, passed a harsher judgement: "He's boring, no conversation." Bearing this in mind, he still commissioned a silk-screen portrait of Yves Saint Laurent for the sum of 25,000 francs.

Karl Lagerfeld was never portrayed by this artist, who was later described as 'the brilliant mirror of our time'. But he remembered what Warhol taught him, better than anyone else.

Karl had front-row seats to Warhol's sophisticated behaviour, his habit of hijacking images and subverting conventions, and his sense of what was not yet known as 'communication'.

Henceforth, Karl set out to enrich his personality. He began strewing his conversation with aphorisms as Warhol did, who published his own regularly in the form of small books. Like Warhol, Lagerfeld sought out accessories which would make him instantly recognisable. Warhol had his peroxided wig; Lagerfeld inaugurated his new outfit with a large fan in painted silk, bought when he was in Japan. He also wore a monocle, which made him look like a Belle Époque baron. He soon grew out his hair, so that he could tie it back with a bow.

Even his German accent was cultivated. During the 1960s, his first radio interviews bear witness to this – it was much less pronounced. Later he began to speak faster, emphasising the staccato delivery that identified him from the very first word. He began to receive invitations to appear on television, where his appearance always caused a sensation. In Rome, where he went regularly to design the Fendi collection, he witnessed an accident one day. Imagine the face of the policemen when Karl arrived to give evidence, wearing a Cerruti hat over his long hair and a fox fur cape, worn over a suit with a floppy necktie and patent leather shoes! He was admired, or perhaps laughed at – it did not matter, so long as he was noticed. "Don't pay attention to what they write about you," Warhol had told him. "Just measure it in inches."

6

Karl Lagerfeld's reputation had not yet spread around the globe, but his adventures with Warhol gave him an aura in the world of fashion that he had hitherto been lacking. The sublime dresses he designed for Chloé always sold well, but now people saw him as an aristocrat of the underground. He played along with it. He had always allowed a measure of doubt to surround his origins: Was he Swedish? The son of a Westphalian baron? These little half-truths were quoted so frequently in the magazines that he must have been their source. Finally, his success was followed by celebrity: the kind that aroused both envy and desire.

When he dined at Le Sept with his little gang, as much attention was paid to his table as was paid to Saint Laurent's, or to the table reserved for Andy Warhol. The 'look' promoted by the boys and girls who surrounded him became more extraordinary every evening. They wore outrageous make-up, swaying and teetering on platform heels, as carefree as young gods. On some evenings, when champagne and excitement flowed freely, Donna Jordan would dance on the table. Beneath her platinum hair and pale face with its plucked-out eyebrows, her gorgeous body was all that was visible, swaying wildly.

Stunning models always followed in Antonio Lopez's wake. Jerry Hall, a long, lean fifteen-year-old blonde, spent all the cash from an insurance claim paid to her after a car accident, to reach Paris; no-one could stand in the way of her fun. She took photos all day, danced every night and shared her apartment with Grace Jones – then a tall, athletic black girl of eighteen – and Jessica Lange, another diaphanous, gentle blonde who dreamed of becoming an actress. Juan Ramos had a new lover: Paul Caranicas, a Greek-American painter who spent his time drawing provocative male nudes in pastel or watercolour. When he wasn't completely high – on a mixture of alcohol and tranquillizers – Corey became less and less of a model and more of a make-up artist for film shoots. Before they hit the latest fashionable nightclub, he would paint the girls' (and the boys') faces in their apartment's tiny bathroom.

The Saint Laurent clan still remained the smartest, and the most attractive. An elegant menagerie clustered round Loulou de la Falaise and Betty Catroux. They included the actor Pascal Greggory and the photographer François-Marie Banier, the faithful Anne-Marie Muñoz (whose son was also Karl's godson), the decorator Jacques Grange, Clara Saint and Thadée Klossowski. Pierre Bergé ruled this little world – but Saint Laurent, despite his delicate nervous system, drew all the looks. Sometimes they met 'outsiders' like the Japanese designer Kenzo, who was preparing to open his second boutique in Paris.

He was amusing, with his flower-strewn fashion and the dances he hosted in his basement, where everyone used to gather after midnight. Lagerfeld's group seemed always on the brink of the craziest adventures: the girls dressed in exotic dresses, lent to them by Karl so that his work might captivate everyone's eyes. At Le Sept, when the two dress designers dined at adjacent tables with their followers, there was always an atmosphere of heightened sexuality and exaltation.

The décor contributed massively. From the outside, Le Sept looked like nothing, with its small, black, unwelcoming door. Guests had to ring the bell, at which point a moustachioed gentleman – the 'physio' – would open up. A long corridor with banquettes stretched along the club's length, with a few cubicles – including the DJ's – and a bar, which could only accommodate a hundred people at a time. "The great thing was the neon lighting," I was told by the designer Vincent Darré. "There were lights on the ceiling in different colours: yellow, pink, mauve, green, which went on and off to the rhythm of the music. Everything was reflected in this room full of neon lights and mirrors. Mixed with the disco music played by Guy Cuevas, everyone quickly went crazy and felt very dizzy…"

Loulou de la Falaise and the models from Saint Laurent, Kenzo and Lagerfeld could sometimes all be found on the tiny tables, dancing with their skirts up to the music of the Dim lingerie advertisements – *Papapapapapam* – in which some of the girls had appeared. It was unusual, nevertheless, to move from one group to another. There was no explicit rule against it – but watch out anyone thinking of taking the risk. The two designers exercised their own unspoken interdict.

When they went to the party that Saint Laurent and Bergé threw in Warhol's honour, Corey and Donna were guilty of a betrayal which they were careful to conceal. Karl and Yves could greet each other as they did in the old days, and sometimes even share a joke, but their followers had to stay put. Referencing Zola's book, *The Sin of Abbé Mouret,* 'The Sin of Pierre Bergé' irritated Lagerfeld, who accused this businessman of keeping his dress designer lover cooped up in a cage. He found Bergé's arrogance and haughtiness irksome, and his way of praising Saint Laurent to the skies as if he had invented him was difficult to bear. "He is not the one with the talent," Karl would mutter, when he heard Bergé holding forth at the next table.

A few exceptional people were welcome in both groups. Picasso and Françoise Gilot's daughter, Paloma, came into their world at the age of twenty, with her Spanish good looks, her blood-red mouth and her potentially fabulous heritage. She clearly had access to anything and everything. Behind his Nikon, Helmut Newton enjoyed the same privileges.

Newton was the most prominent fashion photographer at the time. All the models fought tooth and nail to pose for his stylised photographs, marked as they were with eroticism, both ironic and dark. Like Karl, Helmut was

German, but his Jewish origins had forced him to escape Berlin in 1938 when he was eighteen. He left his father behind, dispossessed of his business by the Aryan laws; he never saw him again. Later, he took Australian nationality, and was intrigued to see how Lagerfeld dealt with his past.

Newton also had to juggle with the Germany of the 1930s, endlessly playing with its image and its sadomasochistic aesthetic. In 1961, he photographed Saint Laurent's dinner jacket for *Vogue*, modelled by an androgynous young woman with short hair who looked like a dandy from Berlin. He also participated in a campaign showing dresses designed by Karl for Chloé. Although he barely ever photographed men, it was Lagerfeld himself he wanted to record for posterity. Since Karl had grown a black beard and wore a monocle, Newton thought of him as one of the German barons of his youth.

Karl did not object. For the photograph, Karl wore a shirt with a false front and a wing collar, as in the portrait of Walther Rathenau, the German Jewish foreign secretary of the Weimar Republic, who was assassinated in 1922 by an antisemitic organisation. "He was my mother's hero," Lagerfeld would claim. Helmut Newton immediately understood the reference. Karl also wore a black jacket, a spotted silk cravat and his famous monocle. The photographer arrived without fuss, with his films in a plastic bag. He worked fast. Who better than he, nevertheless, to detect behind the aristocratic elegance a certain dark and anxious look, which seemed to be focused on some hidden danger in a corner of the room?

What was this anxiety, which gnawed at Lagerfeld when he seemed so well set on the road to success? In addition to Fendi and Chloé, he was working for about thirty different firms in Japan and a brand of lingerie in the United States, while also designing for Germany. He was in demand everywhere. Even actresses were turning to him. In 1967, Saint Laurent dressed Catherine Deneuve in *Belle de jour*; Karl was asked to design for another film by Buñuel five years later. Was he always to follow in Yves' footsteps?

Stéphane Audran spotted the stylist when she was reading *Elle*. He was featured at the top of an article on the most talented new designers of the moment. Since her husband Claude Chabrol had featured her in his films – *Le Boucher, La Femme infidèle* – Stéphane had become a prominent actress. With her grey-green eyes and slow way of speaking, she embodied the kind of beauty who, behind her good looks, conceals perversity and betrayal – this was often the part her husband had her play. Buñuel offered her another role as a rich, leisured woman, starring beside Delphine Seyrig in *Le Charme discret de la bourgeoisie*. Stéphane wanted Karl to dress her for the whole film. "Does this appeal to you?" she enquired. Of course, Karl immediately answered yes. He asked for the screenplay and, as usual, began tirelessly to draw.

When he next saw Stéphane Audran, he showed her some outfits he had designed, going through the story of the film as if he were the director. "Look, here, you have a scene at a table where you have your back to the camera," he explained. "I am going to make you a dress with three cut-out pieces in the back. They will have eyes only for you…" He certainly knew how to talk to women! On the screen, the actress looks dazzling; her sublime black crepe dress has three cut-out lozenges, which show her bare back right down to her waist.

In the press, Stéphane Audran did not forget to mention Karl. Claude Chabrol so admired his wife in this dress – severe at the front and provocative at the back – that he asked the couturier to make another one, this time for his next film, *Les Noces rouges*. Stéphane was to play an unfaithful housewife who would eventually murder her husband with the assistance of her lover. "You need a detail that symbolises sex and death," Chabrol explained. He had never met a costume designer so well-educated and witty. Lagerfeld dreamed up a classic dress, buttoned up the front. When the actress sat down, a scarlet silk slip could just be glimpsed beneath it.

Even Marlene Dietrich asked the designer to visit her. After all, dressing the Blue Angel was just as prestigious as designing dresses for Catherine Deneuve. Karl was flattered, but in truth, he did not like his German compatriot. Josef von Sternberg's favourite actress was still basking in the success of her legendary films and her behaviour during the war, when she had opposed the Nazis from America – she had emigrated there in 1938. In her apartment in Avenue Montaigne, between the portrait of Ernest Hemingway and the portrait of Jean Gabin – her lover during the 1940s – hung the Medal of Freedom she had received from the Americans in memory of *Lili*

Marlene, which she sang on the road in Europe for fifteen solid months to encourage the soldiers of General Patton's third army as they liberated Europe.

By this time, Dietrich was in her seventies. Although she was elegant and beautiful, she was no longer the *femme fatale* she had been before. When she brought him the design for a dress in the European size 36, to be worn at the recitals she continued to give, he almost had to sew it on to her body. Karl was appalled by the way she would enumerate, quite openly, in German: "We must be clear. Look at me; I've got a flat head, only three hairs on my head, breasts that are too heavy, neck and upper body too short, arms too long, flat stomach and bottom. Around the ankle is passable, but the ends of my feet are hideous."

When the telephone or the intercom rang, she would abandon the Wiener Schnitzel she was cooking for him and imitate the voice of her Spanish maid, shouting to the unfortunate caller that "Madame is out." Karl assured his friends that she was not very nice, but basically, he disliked how human she was: "In German, she is witty, in English she's a star, but in French," he joked, "she's just a housewife."

Karl liked to be surrounded by youth, beauty and luxury. When Gabrielle Aghion failed to give him enough money to sustain the reputation of the Chloé collection, he would fill the gap. "I want to be responsible for the creation of the catwalk show, for the publicity and the shop windows – for everything that encourages women to push open the door," he decreed. He insisted on the best-known photographers for the magazines – Helmut Newton, Richard Avedon and Guy Bourdin – and chose whichever models were currently the most popular. He was obsessive about constant change: the great stimulus to fashion.

In his circle, Corey and Pat found their inspiration in artificial stimulants, descending every evening into alcohol and drugs. At Le Sept, little blue or pink Mandrax tablets were passed between the tables. Mandrax acted as a nerve suppressant and could keep you on a high for hours. Everyone around him used drugs. Karl, however, maintained his puritan discipline – his "Prussian backbone," as he used to call it. It did not prevent him from being cheerful, talkative and ready to laugh. He also liked dancing; he did not have the exuberance of Juna and Antonio, but he still had fun. He always remained alert, on the look-out for pretty girls to whom he would present a dress – so that he might later dress them in his collections, like his own personal advertising agents.

There was no-one who could digest, synthesise and transform a detail spotted in the street or on the tiny dance floor at Le Sept into an idea for a dress or a floaty shirt in quite the same way as Karl. He had retained the habit, taught to him by Antonio Lopez, of buying dozens of books every day. He often bought two copies: one for his library, the other for cutting up or underlining as an aid to his work. Films, television and street life were also image banks for him. He absorbed, created and moved on to the next project. "I'm a kind of vampire," he explained. "I drink the blood of others."

There was a new face in his circle. Anna Piaggi was from Milan, a fashion correspondent for Italian *Vogue*. She was small, rather ugly, very witty, sarcastic and crazily eccentric. The hats she dared to wear! The colours she wore together! Anything was permissible in her fashion book. On the telephone she spoke like a serious, well-educated middle-class woman, but when she arrived anywhere her appearance always provoked a gasp of surprise, sometimes laughter. She was a mixture of grotesque and sublime: she might wear billowing trousers, a chicken's foot as a necklace, prominently visible underwear and a little Sumo wrestler's bun on the top of her head.

"My job is to inspire Karl," she liked to say. Karl himself commented that "The way she dresses today automatically forecasts the way we shall be dressing tomorrow." At least his vampire theory was clearly understood by them both. Each detail of her eccentric apparel became a new idea when drawn by Karl. As a result of their friendship, he introduced lace insets into Chloé's dresses and began designing bags and jewellery.

When Karl went to Rome to design the new Fendi collections, Anna accompanied him as his muse, essential to recharge his ideas. At the time, there were no faxes or computers, and he had sometimes to spend several days correcting, adjusting and completing the look. Anna inspired him and made him laugh – and she carried about her person the civilising breath of Italy.

His new friend did not treat him with the careless irony which Corey, Juan or Caranicas allowed themselves these days. Karl continued to work fruitfully with Antonio, but now that the Chloé collections enjoyed new success every year, Lagerfeld reaped the benefits and their relations were strained. The confident liberty of the early days was gone. Antonio and Juan had each found an apartment and were able to escape the couturier's iron control. They had both realised that it was better to be wary of Karl's generosity. Corey, Pat and Jordan were all making an effort to live by their own resources as well. Now that they were not so dependent, they felt free to mock him in a way they would not have previously dared to do. A few months previously, they had not laughed at his high-heeled, black patent mules or the red thigh boots he sported one day in Milan. Now they saw him through new eyes and found him ridiculous.

Lagerfeld was not taken down by the disintegration of his little band. He was well aware of this parade of spongers, when they visited the sumptuous house he continued to rent in Saint-Tropez. The suppressed laughter when he arrived with his monocle and his fan. Perhaps this is the end of an era, he mused. He looked outside of his circle for inspiration.

The years post-1968 proved to be a delightful interlude. Never had anyone enjoyed such complete sexual freedom. At Le Sept, and in dozens of other nightclubs that were flourishing at the time, everyone seemed to be sleeping with everyone else. Girls with boys, girls with girls, boys with boys, transgender people and transvestites wearing outrageous make-up, all mixed and matched in a feeding frenzy of discovery and pleasure.

Gay men, most of all, no longer had to hide. In the world of couture, they had always been there, but were politely not singled out for mention. Christian Dior concealed his homosexuality from the public and his clients right to the end, as if they could not guess, or would not admit it.

It had only been fifteen years, but how much had changed! In the evenings, when they went to have supper at Le Sept or to dance at Le Nuage, Karl would sometimes point out that the majority of the clientele were 'gay', as people in Paris were starting to call it. This was a movement that grew on the dance floor: first with rock, then disco, then an amazing mixture of funk, pop and psychedelic.

Lagerfeld himself relished the sensuality of men, without doubt – even though he liked nothing better than dressing women's bodies. But sex did not interest him. This was the subject of endless jokes between Antonio and Juan: "He never fucks." Around him, loving couples were forming – for the evening, or for the long haul. But no-one had ever known Karl to have any kind of relationship...

7

Looking like a pre-war dandy, with his narrow moustache, his wide-lapelled jackets and a silk scarf round his neck, Jacques could have been a character out of Proust or Oscar Wilde, somewhere between Swann and Dorian Gray. There was a strange glint in his eye, nonetheless; something provocative and perverse.

A good-looking young man, Jacques was the son of minor landed gentry, who lived like turn-of-the-century countryfolk of independent means. 'Jacques de Bascher de Beaumarchais' – that was how he introduced himself, adding the name of a French dramatist to his family name, plus a perfectly appropriated second 'noble particle'. He had no money, although he was keen to give the impression that he had. In fact, he worked intermittently as a cabin steward for Air France, and spent the rest of his time on the lookout for adventure.

Jacques de Bascher had been trying to obtain an introduction to Lagerfeld for months. Time after time, he failed to approach him at the Café de Flore, after parking his motor scooter next to the couturier's midnight blue Bentley. One evening he brought Philippe Heurtault to

Le Sept, a friend from his military days; he pointed out a table where a man was dining with a group of friends: "See over there? He's a Swedish designer. He will soon be one of the greatest designers – and my boyfriend." If he had been more familiar with the fashion world, Jacques would have recognised Antonio Lopez and the little group of Americans surrounding Karl. Try as he might with his carefully chosen clothes, he had no entry into that world. It was really only Lagerfeld and his growing success that caught his eye.

Nobody knows how he wangled it, but Jacques learned that Karl would be at Le Nuage, a small Parisian nightclub about the size of a bathroom, one evening in the summer of 1972. Guy de Cuevas was at the turntable, soon to be headhunted for Le Sept and Le Palace. In the cubicles, a whole menagerie in wigs and leather sipped champagne, surrounded by the sweet smell of poppers.

Bascher had prepared his appearance with great care. "When bent on seduction he left nothing to chance," Heurtault told me. Over a white shirt, the young man wore *lederhosen*, the Tyrolian leather shorts with braces that Lagerfeld had loved since his childhood, and a French navy cap with a red pompom on his head. Nothing grotesque – quite the reverse, he looked charming.

Karl was thirty-eight. He had never met a young man like Jacques: twenty-one, handsome, well educated and enigmatic. Like him, Jacques was a keen reader of Proust and Huysmans, but he also knew the history of the Chouans – a subject venerated by this young aristocrat to the extent that he had had a fleur-de-lis tattooed on his buttock. He spoke English and German fluently, which meant a lot to Lagerfeld, who often used to declare that "people who are not at least trilingual are country bumpkins." It is from this that their unusual love affair developed.

When speaking of Jacques, Lagerfeld used to frequently say: "He was the most stylish Frenchman I have ever seen." Also: "I adored Jacques, but he was impossible." Bascher was indeed handsome and stylish, yet there was also always a glint of cynicism and melancholy in his eye. He worked in dilettante fashion. "I'm writing the screenplay for a film about Gilles de Rais," he would claim – although no-one had ever read more than a few pages of this script about Joan of Arc's companion-in-arms, who had been condemned for heresy, sodomy and the murder of 'at least one hundred and forty children.' But Jacques was generally let off the hook, thanks to his grace and drop-dead attractiveness. "The devil made a man with the head of Garbo," as Lagerfeld was to comment later.

That evening in 1972, Karl's band were unaware of the young man's ploy. Corey, Juan and Antonio only discovered it a few days later, when they retired to the opulent villa rented by Lagerfeld in Saint-Tropez for the third year running. They had never seen their mentor accompanied by a man who looked so much like a conquest. "As soon as Jacques arrived, we understood," Corey remembered. "He totally, completely monopolised Karl's attention." That evening, Corey had to give up his bedroom to the newcomer.

The following day, Juan Ramos and Paul Caranicas were made to leave the villa. Juan, whose eye and taste still won Karl's greatest respect, made fun of their host too openly after this new lover entered their group. "We took too many liberties; we had fun all day while he worked; he'd had enough," Corey explains, adding another reason: "Suddenly Jacques seemed much more inspiring to him than we did." The others stayed on; Antonio in particular continued drawing for Karl. But Jacques, this young man who did nothing but lounge by the pool all day and strike poses, was clearly ready to single-handedly replace the couturier's little band of followers.

When he returned to Paris, Karl did what he always did: he suggested he should put Jacques up in a small bachelor flat in Rue du Dragon. It was a studio flat, completely renovated, with big mirrors hiding the cupboards. Jacques hung up a photograph of the Pope and installed his books, very pleased to be leaving his parents' ground floor apartment in Neuilly, opposite the Bois de Boulogne. Lagerfeld dressed him, too. He designed about twenty silk crepe shirts, which were made by the Italian firm Cifonelli, and gave Jacques half of them. He ordered made-to-measure suits from Caraceni and Renoma, paid for Jacques's social life and showered him with gifts. In the small world of fashion, where everyone knows everything, the situation was soon summed up: "He's Karl's gigolo."

This wasn't incorrect. Karl found it impossible not to ensnare people he loved with his generosity. He paid for everything and Jacques, who had always dreamed of a life of leisure and pleasure, did not resist. This wasn't what Antony and Armelle de Bascher had hoped for their son. Since they returned from Saigon, where Jacques was born, in 1955, they had attempted to instil into their five children the same 'old French' education that they themselves had received. The children had to address their parents with the formal '*vous*' and tutoring in the arts was compulsory – as was participation in the cult of the Château de la Berrière, near Nantes, where the entire family gathered during the summer holidays. This property, rebuilt in the nineteenth century with its moat and fine park, was not only the background to their holidays, it also bred in Jacques the strong illusion that life under the Ancien Régime was the only life worth living.

Monsieur de Bascher was an executive with Shell, who had previously been a colonial civil servant. At one time, he had hoped that his penultimate child would concentrate on his studies. However, Jacques became infatuated with his young English teacher at secondary school: a dandy who drove a Jaguar and introduced his pupil to elegance, literature and homosexuality. After this, Antony 'Tony' de Bascher imagined that national service in the navy would teach him discipline. This adventure only lasted seven months. Jacques was discharged after a number of provocations, and from this chapter in his life he retained only the friendship of Philippe Heurtault and the French navy cap with the red pompom that helped him seduce Karl. After that, 'Tony' made do with giving his son money, but their relationship was cold. No wonder

Jacques was so pleased to have found a sponsor, a protector and a lover... who wasn't one.

Jacques was perfectly aware of the effect he produced. Each time he entered La Coupole or Flore, heads swivelled to watch him cross the room. His fine features – straight nose, light eyes and sensual mouth – were not all that marked him out; it was his way of giving all his energy, his beauty and his time to seduction without any apparent effort.

Danger and surprise were Jacques's constant companions. He was never anywhere he was expected to be, and seemed perpetually on the edge of a precipice. He collected lovers, broke hearts and ruined reputations like a Don Juan – or more accurately, like a courtesan.

One day, Philippe Heurtault was riding a motorcycle down the Rue de Rennes with his friend. "A cop stopped us. Jacques was not wearing a helmet and had left the Harley's papers behind. I went to the house to fetch them. When I came back, they were talking and smiling amicably. The cop did not charge us. To thank him, Jacques invited him home for a drink. He was wearing a wedding ring, I remember. Jacques slept with him that very afternoon."

Karl was not interested in sex. It may even have frightened him. Temperamentally, he was cold, distant and secretive. He might bestow delicate attentions upon a man, but he never allowed so much as a squeeze of the arm, and certainly never any expressions of emotion. Jacques's risk-taking, his creation of a sadomasochistic atmosphere, his taste for the albums of Tom of Finland

and the muscular, leather-clad bikers he brought back from his trips – Karl was amused by the gay aesthetic. But was it worth wasting one's energy on 'going to bed together'? After a few weeks, Jacques realised that his new friend wasn't interested in his body. This was so unusual that he was even more bowled over.

Meanwhile Lagerfeld was in love. Profoundly and absolutely in love. No-one had ever witnessed him so infatuated with another person. He and Jacques would arrive as a couple at Le Sept, where they dined every evening in spite of the restaurant's exorbitant prices. They made a devilishly elegant couple: one with his beard and monocle like a German baron; the other with his inspired outfits, a striped tee shirt over leather trousers one day, a dinner jacket with an open-necked shirt the next. With his confident instinct for attraction, Jacques quickly grasped how he could hold sway over Karl: he would be his black prince, his muse, his spy from the world of the night. Sublimated love.

Jacques de Bascher possessed one precious attribute that fashion always sought: he epitomised his period. Liberty, insolent youth, a taste for sex, dancing, drugs – he had it all in spades. In contrast, Karl was a workaholic, fanatical about discipline, and always watching for anything new. 'Vice paired with virtue' – that was how this compatible duo was viewed.

Jacques was very French, but he claimed to like Germany more than Karl, who was so very German. He dreamed of the romantic history of Ludwig II of Bavaria, venerated the Kaiser and flirted with the decadence of Berlin in the 1920s. Once he came home, delighted with his latest purchase: a Wehrmacht helmet, which he paraded around in naked, or wearing only immaculate white pants, like Charlotte Rampling in *The Night Porter*. When his mentor encouraged him to read Eduard von Keyserling, a Proustian writer who died in Munich a little over century ago, this little aristocrat from the Vendée thought he'd found his ideal world. "The Helmts were so distinguished they could hardly live," von Keyserling wrote. This must have seemed wonderfully similar to Des Esseintes, the hero of *À rebours* by Huysmans, a book Jacques loved.

Perhaps it is strange that Jacques should symbolise the liberated 1970s: he who loved the speeches of Charles Maurras and the Action Française, who declared himself to be a royalist and unashamedly right wing. Even when dead drunk, he would kiss the hand of a married woman, ever observant of etiquette. It was this mixture of contradictions that amused Karl.

In the evenings, Jacques cruised along the Rue Sainte-Anne, dressed in a black leather biker jacket decorated on the back with the Chouan motto '*Ma foy, mon roy*', outlined in studs inside a Vendéen heart. He would get up late, at about 2pm, to go to the cinema, stopping on the way back to play pinball in a café. When Lagerfeld returned at the end of the afternoon, Jacques always had an adventurous story to tell, or an interesting observation to make. According to Paquita Paquin, the former people-watcher of The Palace, "Karl needed this expert on nocturnal activity, who saw how people dressed and kept him informed of the trends."

Being supported by Karl had its obligations. 'Jako', as Karl called him, could make as many conquests as he liked – but he had to be available at all times, which meant dining almost every evening with Karl. Karl was a protector on whose finance Jacques depended for everything – his social life, his clothes and the IBM ball typewriter which Karl refused to buy for him. One day *L'Orage*, the navy ship on which Jacques had done his national service, was due to dock in Brest. Jacques wanted to drive there in a Rolls-Royce to tease the officers who had dismissed him. Lagerfeld refused to indulge this whim. "He did not want Jacques to act independently," suggested Philippe Heurtault.

This was almost certainly true. Being maintained puts a person in a delicate position: he must be endlessly watchful and endlessly desirable to avoid the danger of being abandoned. Jacques swallowed these little humiliations like a child submitting to the authority of his father. He was far too pleased at having a platonic lover who was as familiar with his up-market clients as he was with the crazy nightclubs Jacques frequented. When he brought a young man back to his flat, he would often play him a recording of the stylist's voice – so recognisable with its German accent – or if Karl telephoned, he would pass the receiver to his boyfriend of the moment.

Everything was permitted during the 1970s. Although Karl only ever drank Coca-Cola, Jacques plunged head first into the current range of drugs. As soon as he woke up, he would sniff a line of cocaine. In the evening he would take a Mandrax which, accompanied by Chivas drunk straight from the bottle, hugely increased his erotic sensibility. He would have to have been no more than twenty in order to sustain this frenzied, destructive routine without apparent damage. He wanted to live without thought for the future, however, and what other duty did he have but fun? "Jacques's job was being Jacques," – this was the observation of Karl's friend from Hamburg, Florentine Pabst. He would spend hours getting ready before he went out. Then he would painstakingly ruin his careful arrangement as the evening wore on. This was the complete opposite of Lagerfeld, who could always be found at home in a white piqué dressing gown, drawing for Fendi, Chloé and the many other labels that employed him on a freelance basis.

One evening, Jacques met Diane de Beauvau-Craon, a descendant of one of the most illustrious French families, who were related to the Counts of Anjou and the Dukes of Lorraine. Jacques, always so keenly aware of pedigrees, was immediately fascinated by the clash between her family tree and her behaviour. With her crew-cut hair and her androgynous figure, the fifteen-year-old Diane always had the look of a devilish young man, crazy and entertaining, as indolent as Jacques and just as much of a junkie. Three days after their first meeting, they made an appointment in the flat in Rue du Dragon. "He was infernally handsome, and drop dead attractive," she remembers. What did it matter if he preferred men? This 'fag hag', as she described herself, went out with Jacques every evening. In the clubs where they danced, people began to suspect her of pimping for him, as they attracted the attention of so many young men.

The couple lived dangerously, always on the brink of overdose or scandal. Karl Lagerfeld eventually telephoned Diane's father and asked him to "look after his daughter" after Jacques had played truant on yet another night. "It wasn't that Karl was jealous, or possessive. He was afraid I would harm Jacques," Diane said, recently. And Karl was right. Jacques had no fear of anything: neither the law, nor death, nor any taboos.

The two clans often rubbed shoulders at Le Sept. In the restaurant, you might bump into Michel Guy, the future Minister of Culture; the Rothschilds; or Françoise Sagan playing cards with the beautiful Peggy Roche, her mistress, who was a fashion journalist before she became a stylist. Mick Jagger or David Bowie might be dancing in the club, accompanied by a bevy of models who gave the evening the fun and sparkle that the licentious guests were looking for.

Jacques moved easily between two worlds. At dinner time, he sat at Karl's table. He always had a funny story to tell, and all the latest gossip. Around midnight, they went down to the basement, where people drank champagne around the dance floor. From the bar, Jacques eyed the different groups with (fake) detachment. He was very conscious that he too was being watched.

Jacques liked nothing better than to disrupt people's security and sow disarray. One day a good-looking man was pointed out to him, a man sure in his taste for women. Jacques immediately wanted to see him succumb to his charm – after which he would summarily abandon him, gasping with desire. Lagerfeld loved it when 'Jako' would entertain him with the foibles of a certain society figure the following day, or relate intimate gossip about a night-time celebrity. This was how Karl possessed others: through his intermediary.

8

Idleness was unthinkable. When he wasn't working, Jako spent every day looking for entertainment, a new surprise, something to add spice to his life. Gathering lovers did not really interest him: "He was excited by the impossible," suggested his friend, Philippe Heurtault. And the impossible, the unthinkable, the only forbidden fruit had a name: Saint Laurent.

It could have been a modern farce. Two former friends, reduced to a lover and the husband who hides in the wardrobe. Although it was clandestine at the outset, the relationship that Jacques de Bascher was about to embark upon with Karl's rival couturier would soon run out of control and shake the small world of fashion to its foundations, far more deeply than Jacques could have anticipated.

Relations between Yves and Pierre Bergé had been evolving for some time. Their parties were always the most opulent; dozens of works of art adorned the elegant duplex and eight hundred square metres of garden at 55 Rue de Babylone, where they moved in 1972. The couple were certainly wealthy, but more than that, they personified the successful, attractive elite; they were the 'beautiful people' of the day. Since the death of Coco Chanel, Balenciaga and Schiaparelli, Saint Laurent seemed to be the only remaining 'French star' of haute couture. He sketched free and independent women, who strode along in floaty trousers and silk muslin shirts. Saint Laurent himself often wore a white dinner jacket, like the Great Gatsby. He was a good-looking man, thirty-seven years old.

By now, Bergé had fully assumed the role of producer and director. It was he who prepared the transfer of the couture house from Rue Spontini to Avenue Marceau. With his grey suits, he always looked like a businessman – and this is undoubtedly what he was. The development of the haute couture business was all his work, as was the ready-to-wear line and the perfumes. He looked after his 'genius' partner like a nursemaid – Yves, who seemed so far removed from the real world that he couldn't buy an air ticket.

It was not always easy. Saint Laurent could switch from intense excitement to the darkest depression, intoxicated by success and then devastated by his critics. Like an adolescent, he was keen to escape the iron grip of his companion, who nevertheless ensured his liberty by taking care of his affairs. In public, Yves treated Pierre very casually, allowing his friends to make fun of him behind his back. In private, he set out to increase the number of his conquests, always with that fake prudishness that adds a delicious frisson to sex.

He had noticed the young De Bascher when he arrived in Lagerfeld's circle. How could he not? The two clans spent almost every evening at adjacent tables in Le Sept. In Spring 1973, the entire small world of fashion had seen the pictures of Jako posing beside Karl in the new apartment Karl had rented on the second floor of a building in Place Saint-Sulpice. The flat was painted entirely black and white. Measuring three hundred and ninety square metres, it was just above the level of the chestnut trees in flower, with a view of the fountain and the fabulous church. It was furnished with Art Deco pieces: a superb pair of Dunand vases and two console tables by Eugène Printz, bought in the salerooms at which both Bergé and Lagerfeld were customers. The pair would occasionally cross paths there and exchange elaborate greetings.

Antonio Lopez and Juan Ramos returned to New York in 1974. After that, Karl took Jacques everywhere. They dressed in the same style: jackets with broad lapels and trousers with turn-ups, with silk blousons and foulards round their necks (and sometimes, in Jako's case, a cream linen suit, again like Gatsby). With his narrow moustache and, in summer, his straw Borsalino, Jacques modelled his look on Robert de Montesquiou, the dandy who was Huysman's inspiration for Des Esseintes. Jacques often carried around Philippe Jullian's biography of Huysman.

Obsessed with the aristocracy, his dream was to lead the life of the old landed gentry – or their life as he imagined it to be. He had tried in vain to convince Lagerfeld to pay for repairs to the Château de la Berrière, but Karl had no desire to be attached to another man's family, although he always treated Armelle de Bascher with impeccable courtesy.

One day, however, Jacques organised a weekend in Brittany to show Karl a *château* in the Morbihan that happened to be for sale. The fashion world soon learnt that Lagerfeld, the stylist from Chloé, had bought this property, which his boyfriend so adored. The Château de Penhoët was a handsome house in Grand-Champ, built of pale granite, about fifteen kilometres from Vannes. "The overall effect was much more of a private residence in the Rue de Varenne than a castle in Brittany" – this was Lagerfeld's opinion. He was amused to see Jacques immediately busy himself with redesigning the park in the French manner, allotting the bedrooms and planning parties and balls. Karl entered into the spirit of the endeavour, asking Patrick Hourcade – a former history of art student who worked at *Vogue*, introduced to him by Anna Piaggi – to help him restore the property to its former glory. Hourcade, a handsome young man who loved architecture, gave Karl the following advice: "Before you touch your house, look in the archives and books at the aesthetic of the period." "Could you do it for me?" And so, work at Grand-Champ continued for months.

On Hourcade's advice, workmen blew up tree roots and dug stone ponds. Lime trees and shrubs were planted and Pouter pigeons installed in the dovecote. The house itself was entirely renovated, its forty rooms redecorated with chests-of-drawers, beds and console tables from the auction rooms. It was very late seventeenth, early eighteenth-century: Karl's favourite period – he always claimed to find nothing more beautiful than the Château de Versailles. On the ground floor, a series of drawing rooms welcomed the guests. Jacques's bedroom was in the attic, as charming as the bedroom of a cherished son. Between the two, on the first floor, Karl's rooms were on the left and Elisabeth's on the right.

Elisabeth Lagerfeld adored Grand-Champ the minute she saw it, and work on her bedroom had to be hurried so that she could move in as soon as possible. She spent hours up there, listening to music, reading the paper and drinking tea. Grand-Champ became a family home once more, the joint project of Karl and Jacques building themselves an intimate space. Why would De Bascher risk ruining everything?

Yves should have stopped himself succumbing. He had many happy memories of Karl, when they used to laugh until dawn, lying on either side of Victoire. Although the relationship between Bergé and Karl had always contained a sour note, Yves and Karl understood and even admired each other. Of course, Saint Laurent's fame was sky high by now – but he recognised Lagerfeld's talent for design, his inventiveness and his formidable sense of the period and awareness of change. Jacques was at once impossible to contemplate and impossible to resist.

At the end of 1973, Yves sent his friend Clara Saint to invite the forbidden fruit to one of his catwalk shows. A few weeks earlier, on 10 September, Karl had celebrated his fortieth birthday by inviting the entire Saint Laurent clan. A little photograph appeared in *Vogue,* proving that they were all there: Bergé, Loulou de la Falaise, Paloma

Picasso, Thadée Klossowski and Clara Saint. They all look a bit sulky, except for Yves, who appears delighted. Was there already something in the air?

Who knew that Saint Laurent had fallen madly in love with Jacques? Very few people. Clara, of course, who had acted as their go-between. Philippe, Jacques's friend, who witnessed the heaps of white flowers that Yves sent daily to the small apartment in Rue du Dragon. For the rest, the lovers conducted their affair in secret.

On 25 February 1974, the Bergé-Saint Laurent couple gave another party in honour of Warhol in Rue de Babylone. The opening of the Mao exhibition, featuring paintings and silk screen prints by the Great Helmsman of China himself, had taken place three days earlier and, as happened every time Andy came to Paris, the event caused a sensation. The *Tout-Paris* of fashion and art had been invited.

That both Lagerfeld and De Bascher were in attendance indicates that relations between the two clans were still good. Philippe Heurtault was invited, on the instigation of Jacques – he was the only photographer present that evening. With his small camera, he managed to capture Warhol and the English painter David Hockney, who invited Jacques to pose for him, then Paloma Picasso and François-Marie Banier. For posterity, he also recorded Karl and Jacques, Karl and Yves, and Jacques and Pierre, as if no-one yet knew what was going on behind the scenes – which was indeed the case. In the photographs, Jako allays suspicion perfectly. Looking very elegant in his black suit and large-collared shirt, he clasps Pierre Bergé's shoulder as if they're the best of friends. Yves does the same with Karl, one amicable hand placed on the neck of his former friend, now rival.

In the photographs where Yves and Jacques appear together, on the other hand, Saint Laurent looks haggard. "When drunk, he seemed hardly in control and would stand there, fascinated, in front of Jacques," remembers Philippe Heurtault. Saint Laurent continuously replenished his own glass. He could hardly stand up, and Jacques was anxious that a gesture or an inadvertent cry would give the game away. Suddenly – a loud bang. Saint Laurent had fallen over, bringing down one of the two narwhal tusks that adorned the entrance to the apartment. Scandal was averted. For tonight, at least, no-one would suspect anything.

Karl was soon to be in the know, however. Did Jacques confess or did Karl guess? "Jealousy is for the middle classes," the designer would always maintain. He must have been hurt by the intrigue, all the same, with its overtones of symbolic betrayal. He did not let his feelings show, simulating indifference. He did, however, alert Jacques to the perils of the scheme. Yves was not just any lover. He was celebrated and the image of his business was linked to his own image – an image Pierre Bergé had his eye on.

Did Jako love his new conquest? No certainty there. But he was definitely flattered. After Karl introduced him to Andy Warhol, he bought a Polaroid SX70 and a cassette recorder, the same model lugged around by the prince of Pop Art. As with his other suitors, Jacques recorded Yves and played his fervent declarations of love to Philippe Heurtault. "Listen, it's a historic declaration!" he would say, laughing like a child.

Jacques was unrivalled in his ability to imagine scenarios and invent disguises that played to Saint Laurent's erotic masochism. He dressed as a cherub one day, a German soldier the next. Yves called him "my lieutenant", and was charmed at being ordered to submit – he, whom the world held in such adulation. Nothing stopped Jacques, not even when the couturier put his signet ring on the electric hob to mark Jacques's buttock with his seal.

Saint Laurent's friends were familiar with the couturier's passions and sudden infatuations. Yves could spend a whole night pursuing a young man he fancied, then cause a disturbance and end up at the police station; Pierre Bergé always arrived with his cheque book to repair the damage. But going out with Jacques was something else. Jacques was a perverse character who knew neither checks nor boundaries. He played schoolboy tricks, like the time at Brasserie Lipp when he bombarded the society dancer Jacques Chazot with little pornographic messages, pretending they came from another customer who knew nothing of the ploy. But he could also play more dangerous games.

Jacques carried a small gold snuffbox on his person, from Cartier, which was always filled with cocaine. Under his influence, Yves descended into drugs. He would stay up all night, obsessing about the next evening they would spend together. One night they caused such a scandal that

Yves was bundled into a police van, not a penny on him – Jacques watched from behind a bush, doubled up with laughter.

Saint Laurent no longer designed anything, or he would just draw De Bascher wearing the silk blouses Lagerfeld had made for him. One couturier redesigning the creations of another – what a strange descent to rock bottom. Jacques had been looking for a brief affair, but what fell into his arms was unbridled passion. Yves inundated him with letters, stifled him with bouquets of flowers from Lachaume, told him his whole life story, gave him opulent presents and other more intimate gifts – like the little black and white photograph of him, as a child, on a beach in Brittany, below which he wrote: "Yves, the duckling of Concarneau." In short, their affair had consumed him.

At the beginning, Jacques used to laugh about Yves with his friends. Later, he sighed like a Don Juan pursued by an ancient mistress. For a joke, the writer Yves Navarre, one of Jacques's many former lovers, used to telephone his friend and imitate the couturier's drawl, playing on the similarity of their first names: "Hallo? This is Yves…" "Stop, you're scaring me!" Jacques admitted that he was overwhelmed by Yves's all-consuming love. In addition, he was already infatuated with another young man: Alan Cornelius, a handsome American. He purposely pinned up photographs of Alan around his picture of the Pope.

The YSL fashion house could not turn a blind eye to this disorder of which the prince of fashion suffered. He had lost weight. He hardly came to work, and when he did, his face was haggard. Sometimes, Pierre Bergé had to ring round all their friends to find him; he soon pinpointed De Bascher as the source of all the trouble. The affair may have been no more than a sentimental drama, but Karl was right to warn Jacques: Saint Laurent was not just any lover. He represented a fortune, an image, employees. Bergé was forced to admit that everything they had built up together was now under threat.

Up until this time, the clans had intermingled, the goad of latent competition hardly felt. Everyone understood that Saint Laurent was a genius, and Lagerfeld was sufficiently intelligent to appear unmoved by it. But since Yves had begun frantically begging for scraps of attention from Jacques de Bascher, Pierre Bergé got into his head that this young man was the weapon with which Karl intended to destroy his rival. This was not the case; Lagerfeld had organised nothing. But it did have a ring of truth about it, nevertheless. He had allowed it to happen, and each evening would listen attentively with his eyes turned to the ceiling, as Jacques told him about Saint Laurent's descent into hell. "If the flies buzz around the light bulb and burn themselves, it's not my fault," Jacques would intone, like Marlene Dietrich in *The Blue Angel*.

"Jacques would never have left Karl for Yves, simply because there were 36,000 Yves in his life," is the opinion of Diane de Beauvau-Craon today. But Saint Laurent? Could he have abandoned his designs, his dresses, his sublime fashion shows? That was Bergé's fear. He said nothing when his partner bought himself a bachelor flat in Avenue de Breteuil. But now that Yves's all-consuming passion was threatening the collapse of their fashion house, so patiently built up over the years, Bergé intended to retaliate.

Something else bothered him, too. A few months earlier, Jacques had brought one of his protégés to Grand-Champ: José, an awkward young man whom he introduced as a distant cousin. The young man lived in the gatekeeper's lodge at the *château*, kept Elisabeth Lagerfeld company and was supposed to look after the accounts. One day, some money disappeared. José was accused of dishonesty. He was sacked. Three days later, he was found dead a few kilometres away. The young man had committed suicide, throwing himself under a train on a deserted section of railway line near Vannes. He was twenty-eight years old.

Pierre Bergé was horrified by this news. Jacques was dangerous; that much was certain. "Don't see those terrible people anymore," he said, on Yves's orders, to all those – Loulou, Thadée, Jacques Grange – who continued to be De Bascher's friends. Each new event posed a threat. One evening, after an argument, Saint Laurent left in his little black Beetle. Twenty-four hours later, after phoning round all the police stations, Pierre found him in a hospital in the north of Paris. It could not go on.

And so, at Le Sept one evening, Pierre Bergé took Karl aside. "You have to look after your little whore!" he yelled in front of all the amazed guests. "Yves is not your property!" was Lagerfeld's retort. Later, rumour had it that someone had been slapped in the face. This is wrong; the slap was for Jacques, when Bergé happened to bump into him on another evening – but it was obvious to everyone that war had been declared. After fruitless scenes and threats, Pierre Bergé telephoned Jacques and lay down an ultimatum: if he did not leave the couturier, something bad would happen... "This was the most terrifying telephone call Jacques had ever received," said Philippe Heurtault, who heard the recording his friend made of this call.

Perverse Jacques, usually so self-confident, became paranoid. He was convinced that Bergé had dispatched thugs to assassinate him. "He shouted: 'he's sent a team of crack shots to the Tuileries to kill me!'" Philippe told me. The threat was so serious that De Bascher stopped answering Saint Laurent's desperate calls. To be more secure, he gave Yves's letters to Lagerfeld for safekeeping – "letters that couldn't be seen," which Lagerfeld assured me were full of pornographic drawings and obscenities.

One night, when Jacques had been avoiding Saint Laurent's incessant phone calls for a few days, Saint Laurent got into his car completely drunk. He drove round and round Place Saint-Sulpice shouting "Jacques, Jacques!" until the neighbours called the police. That was towards the end of 1975; at that moment, everything that linked the two most famous couturiers of the day was blown to smithereens.

For a long time, Pierre Bergé held De Bascher responsible for all of these troubles: their separation in 1976, Saint Laurent's descent into the inferno of drugs and depression.

"J. de B. was only a pretext," he would later write in his *Lettres à Yves*, 2009, "the opportunity you were looking for and which presented itself." Undoubtedly, this is true – although Yves's heart was not the only one broken in 'J. de B.'s long catalogue of lovers.

Such an incident might have had serious consequences for Jacques. Yes, he was young and handsome, but Diane de Beauvau-Craon emphasised that "It was Karl who pulled the strings." If Lagerfeld sent him packing, Jacques's extravagant lifestyle would end, as would his success at parties and in the magazines. In the world of fashion, most people had been ordered to choose between the two clans: you could no longer be friends with Lagerfeld *and* Saint Laurent.

Jacques, however, managed to maintain his position. Karl took great care to make things clear. In what could have been a message directed at his protégé, as well as to the rumour mill of their little fashion world, he explained in *Interview*, Andy Warhol's magazine: "I never fall in love, I'm in love only with my work". The magazine published photographs of his bedroom in Place Saint-Sulpice, an immense bed covered in maroon fabric with a metal plinth he had designed himself. Alongside was his commentary: "This type of bed was designed for single people. If you consider the piece in its setting, you will think of anything but sex, because the room is as a-sexual as it could be. I love a-sexual bedrooms." If Saint Laurent was consumed by this depraved relationship, Karl demonstrated that he was still firmly in charge of everything.

Elisabeth was not as she had been. She had formerly lived in her apartment in Saint-Sulpice, a huge room whose windows looked out over the corner of Rue des Canettes. Following a stroke, however, Madame Lagerfeld had retreated to Grand-Champ, where Pilar and Rafael, a Spanish couple, were employed to look after her.

Karl hated illness. He avoided his friends when they had even the slightest cold, and never visited his acquaintances in hospital. How would he cope with the sight of his mother in a wheelchair, her memory failing her? When he came to Brittany with Jacques and Anna Piaggi, or even more so when he came with fashion editors or contacts he wanted to impress, Elisabeth remained invisible – shut up in her quarters, where she laid on a sofa and listened to Strauss's Der Rosenkavalier.

Then, one day in 1978, Pilar and Rafael telephoned to say that Madame Lagerfeld had just passed away. The hairdresser had been in the morning, followed by the doctor, who came to prescribe for her persistent cold. The doctor hardly had time to walk across the room before Elisabeth died.

Karl did not visit. He maintained that his mother had always rejected the idea of a funeral ceremony. Only the Spanish couple were at the cremation. The ashes were placed in an urn, which had been specially bought in a saleroom. From now on, Karl could make his mother live as he wished.

9

Karl had one thing in common with Jacques: he liked to re-shape reality to suit his taste, his ideas and his interests. He began by sustaining the vagueness surrounding his father: Swedish, Danish, no-one was clear of his origins. Now that he had crossed the hurdle of forty, he began to lie about his age. No-one gets old in fashion. For the Chloé catwalk shows, Lagerfeld systematically turned down models who were over thirty. At Le Sept, everyone lived, danced and took drugs as if it were not worth conserving themselves for the years to come. How could Karl have admitted how many of those years had passed him by?

In the middle of his life, the couturier also began a physical transformation. He shaved off his beard, abandoned the intensive strength training regime that had given him the figure of a body builder, and put on weight. The fan that he had adopted served him more and more frequently to mask the effects of age and weight gain. Each time he remembered the eighteen-year gap between him and Jako, he felt time gnawing at his neck.

During his first interview with France Inter, in 1958, he openly admitted his age, twenty-five. Thenceforward he readily modified his birth date: 1933… 1935… 1938… He played with the possibilities. This sometimes obliged him to adjust the stories he told so frequently about his past, but he was amused by the little lies that filled the newspapers – no-one ever checked. If he was born in 1938, were his early days not a bit precocious? "At fourteen, I came to Paris and I lived entirely on my own, like an adult," was his grand claim.

About half a dozen photographs and articles still exist documenting the famous fashion competition in 1954, which Lagerfeld won with Yves Saint Laurent. Lagerfeld's age, twenty-one, is openly mentioned, but no-one ever dared put the documents under his nose. "The Jedi have no age," wrote one fashion editor, slightly pompously, as if it was useless to enquire. Even in Germany, where some of his school friends, neighbours and cousins followed his ascent to fame and fortune, the matter was never rectified.

Karl often let those close to him organise birthday parties where there were five too few candles on the cake. If anyone insisted on knowing the truth, he would wriggle out with a side step: "My age? I shall never reveal it, and anyway there are some things even I don't know about myself." Later, when he was over seventy, faced with young people in their twenties during a television broadcast, he repeated his profoundly held certainty: "I don't belong to any generation!" Nevertheless, when the suspicions became more pressing and the lie was about to be revealed, he skirted round the issue, bringing on Madame Lagerfeld in her role as the statue of the Commendatore:

he stated on a number of occasions that "She wanted to change my birth certificate, I don't know why, and after that she burned everything."

Was it at that juncture that he began re-inventing Elisabeth? After the death of his mother, Karl endlessly breathed new life into her. Her jet-black hair, her earrings with the oblong pearl, her small size – 36 or 38. When he described her, it was as if he were redesigning his ideal woman. The hausfrau from Hamburg disappeared behind an elegant silhouette, such as one might have encountered in the society papers of Weimar or Heidelberg.

At the beginning, he simply re-invented the social origins of his parents. In any number of interviews in the 1970s, Otto is a baron, Elisabeth the daughter of the governor of Westphalia. You only have to flip through the thick file of press cuttings from *Le Monde* – fifteen centimetres thick – to get an idea of this fantastical story Karl told: a childhood blown out of proportion. The house in Bad Bramstedt is transformed into a castle, the gleaming stables hold a prize-winning herd of cows. Servants multiply, and his sisters' nanny is transmogrified into a French governess attached to him alone – the super-gifted child. The war does not seem to exist in this landscape, where Lagerfeld apparently enjoyed the childhood of a young lord.

In the middle of this opulent scene, the most highly coloured portraits are reserved for Karl's mother. She is always glamorous, fabulous and wonderfully gifted. "My mother was a violinist…" he claimed in many of his interviews for *Interview*, Andy Warhol's magazine.

"…[S]he often practised for three hours at a stretch in the mornings, on a nineteenth-century German violin, a very rare instrument. She would play quartets with musicians who came to the house. Curiously, she put her violin down one day and never touched it again." Then, for good measure, he would add: "She was a woman who piloted her own aeroplane in 1919, very modern, very liberated." He even claimed one day that he had inherited the Grand-Champ property from his mother, as if it had been in the family for generations. What did truth matter when the newspapers were ecstatic about his extraordinary tales? Swedish, Danish or a German aristocrat, it was a pedigree that suited Jacques de Bascher's fancies as much as it suited the public watching Lagerfeld's first forays into television. He demonstrated an amazing talent for dissolving reality into his home-grown legend.

Over the years, he began to ventriloquise Elisabeth. Madame Lagerfeld, as seen by Karl, was a long series of disobliging comments, repeated with glee. "She always told me that my nostrils were too big and that someone should ring up an upholsterer to make some curtains… And, regarding my hair, which was chestnut-mahogany in colour, 'you look like an antique chest-of-drawers'," he repeated about himself in an interview. He refined his stories, sometimes adding variations: "As a child, I used to wear Tyrolean hats and my mother said to me one day: 'You look like an ancient lesbian.' I was eight. She was witty, wasn't she?" And then: "My mother said: 'He has a fat stomach,' and she made me sleep wearing a belt."

Karl Lagerfeld (21, left) and Yves Saint Laurent (18, centre) debut at a fashion design show organised by Woolmark, 11 December 1954.   Keystone-France / Contributor / Getty

The well-stocked library in Karl's Paris apartment, 13 April 1969.
                              Fairchild Archive / Penske Media / Shutterstock

Jacques de Bascher poses for a portrait at the Advance Preview (part 3) of Chloé's Spring 1974 ready-to-wear collection, 22 October 1973.

Karl dancing with Anna Piaggi at the Ideacomo Ball, Como, Italy, 17 November 1978.

Andy Warhol photographs a group of revellers, including Karl (centre) and Paloma Picasso, at Le Palace nightclub, Paris, 1 January 1980.   Francis Apesteguy / Contributor / Getty

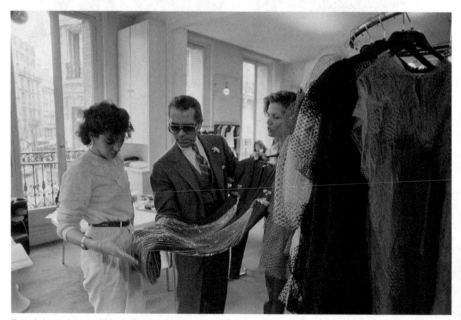

Examining a dress at Chloé's Paris studio, 11 April 1983.

Pierre VAUTHEY / Contributor / Getty

Drawing his designs at Chloé's Paris studio, 11 April 1983.

Fitting one of his designs to Inès de la Fressange, 11 April 1983.

Pierre VAUTHEY / Contributor / Getty

Standing in front of a wall of designs, which document his first year at Chanel, 5 March 1984.

John van Hasselt - Corbis / Contributor / Getty

The famous road safety advertisement campaign, 18 June 2008.

Attending the Dior Menswear Fall/Winter 2016/2017 fashion show at Tennis Club de Paris, 23 January 2016.

Karl walks the runway with his godson Hudson Kroenig, during Chanel's show at Paris Fashion Week Womenswear Fall/Winter 2016/2017, 8 March 2016.　　　　　Victor Boyko / Contributor / Getty

Or: "My mother tried to get me started on the piano. One day she closed the top of the keyboard on my fingers and said: 'Draw. It's less noisy'." The list of "My mother said…", or "My mother thought…" is endless, creating the picture of a terrifying education and a very unusual mother.

In his fantasies, Elisabeth was "always beautifully dressed, so perfect." Nothing like Otto, dismissed in two scathing lines by Karl – or, more frequently, omitted completely. She was a virtuoso violin player, had translated Teilhard de Chardin into German and smoked without worrying. She was pitiless towards her son: "I was born three weeks late. My mother told me that she went to the hospital every day because she didn't want such a 'dirty event' to take place in the house. I have never regained those three weeks." As if to compensate for her harshness, Karl made his sisters Thea and Christel the daughters of Madame Lagerfeld's first marriage, "forgotten in a boarding school in a foreign country." Quite predictably, the couturier was always willing to state "my mother said that, if we are honest with ourselves, psychoanalysis does no-one any good."

Patrick Hourcade, who knew Elisabeth Lagerfeld in Paris and Grand-Champ, remembers a woman who was "well brought up and had a strong sense of propriety." As portrayed by Karl, she becomes subjugating and castrating, highly intelligent but very unmaternal. Why was he so keen to remind us that, when he told her he was going to be a couturier, she replied: "That shows you have no ambition, no drive!" Why did he tell people that she had no interest in his designs and had never been near one of his catwalk shows, when everyone who knew her assures me that she only wore outfits by Sonia Rykiel or, even more often, clothes designed by her son?

He loved these provocative stories that suggested noble birth and a nineteenth-century style education, and which helped paint a fascinating portrait of himself. "Childhood decides," wrote Sartre in *Les Mots*, one of Karl's favourite books. By describing a youth that was like no-one else's, he predisposed other people to agree that the adult he then became was very out of the ordinary.

Saint Laurent always replied to journalists in a whisper, and went so far as to forbid photographers access to his house: "No flash, please." Karl Lagerfeld was the exact opposite. Every time he appeared, he delivered a new episode of his lavish life story, which grabbed public interest while leaving his mysterious side in the shadows.

This is the period when Karl was at his most celebrated. The star of the one o'clock news on television, Yves Mourousi, whom he would meet almost every evening at the bar in Le Sept, urged him to re-style Dani, the oracle of the 1970s, as a vamp. The portraits multiplied. The cosmetics company Elizabeth Arden signed a valuable contract with Chloé for the launch of a new perfume, which would bear Lagerfeld's name. The owners of Chloé, Gabrielle Aghion and Jacques Lenoir, agreed that Karl should have a share in the profits – not of the prêt-à-porter, of which he was already the artistic director, but of the new fragrance. Karl Lagerfeld attended the launch, setting off for the United States with Jacques, where, from Los Angeles to New York, the stories of his childhood, his relationship with De Bascher and his self-assurance in front of the media quickly made him famous.

After her stroke, when Elisabeth left Paris permanently for Grand-Champ, Karl gave her Saint-Sulpice apartment to Jacques. From this time on, he rented first a wing, then the whole of a private residence: the Hôtel Pozzo di Borgo, 51 Rue de l'Université. The Bergé-Saint Laurent couple had been tempted to rent this sumptuous building several years earlier. Lagerfeld decorated it throughout in eighteenth-century style, with gilding everywhere and priceless furniture. With 'Pozzo', he could perfect the invented story of his life.

Awed journalists discovered a suite of drawing rooms that might have been inspired by the Château de Versailles; they were sometimes granted a glimpse of a small bedroom as a surprise. "A four-poster bed in the Polish style, with celadon green hangings matching the curtains… in short, a bijou bedroom which Marie-Antoinette would not have rejected," writes Virginie Mouzat, then fashion editor of *Le Figaro*. "That was my childhood bedroom," Karl assured her.

He also pointed out a small painting on the wall: *The Round Table*, a copy of the painting by Adolph von Menzel, the nineteenth-century artist from Berlin. It shows Frederick II of Prussia surrounded by friends, including Voltaire, who are being received at the castle of Sans-Souci. "I fell in love immediately with this copy of

Menzel's painting," he claimed. Another episode in the fairy tale of his life. According to the various versions, he was five, sometimes seven, when he begged his parents to buy him this copy – or bought it himself, or insisted (a new version) that the shop should be opened especially for him on Christmas Eve, preferring to obtain the painting by hook or by crook, rather than the manservant he had been offered for Christmas! Karl claimed that the painting was sent with the furniture from his childhood bedroom, just after the death of his father. This vision, nurtured by Karl over the years, figures in most of the portraits devoted to him as proof of his precocious brilliance: it is his Rosebud, as well as his key to the life to which he aspired.

Work at the Château de Grand-Champ was finished at last – and the results were spectacular. Karl and Jacques went there nearly every weekend with friends, and sometimes with fashion editors whom the couturier needed to impress. That was where Karl used to work, above the park with its bushes clipped as they were at Versailles, and the new pond he had ordered dug. The guests rose at 10am. He joined them at 1.30pm for lunch – served in fine china, with Baccarat glasses. But for the eccentricity of Anna Piaggi, one might have imagined oneself in the eighteenth century, in the heart of the French court. Karl even dressed in the style of the period; he received his guests in a silk jacket, his hair tied back with a bow like a gentleman of yesteryear.

The country folk in Brittany could not believe their eyes when this group took a walk in the park, or went to mass in a Rolls-Royce on Sundays. Anna in particular caused a sensation: "She took hours getting dressed, then she would arrive in the most improbable outfits which Karl loved to draw," remembers Patrick Hourcade. When Jacques ordered gourmet picnics by the sea on the Ria d'Etel, she wore the most outrageous bathing suits without fear of ridicule. The men did not lag far behind: Jacques always made an event of going for a drink at the café in the 'village' (as he would say, in the condescending tone of an aristocrat talking about the yokels) dressed in a white suit and a Panama hat. One day, Karl bought half a dozen old Chinese silk coats. The little group caused a sensation as they strolled around the park: "The locals mistook Karl for the singer Demis Roussos, at the top of the hit-parade at the time, going for a walk with his courtiers," Hourcade laughed.

One evening, Lagerfeld gave a party on the pale parquet floor of the Rue de l'Université. He wore a white curled wig with the usual black velvet bow behind, a white shirt with a jabot and red breeches, white stockings and gold-buckled black shoes. He designed the staff livery himself. To welcome the guests, his flunkies wore jackets with gold facings, carrying candelabras. On the buffet, reconstituted swans and a peacock, as well as lobsters bearing cornucopias, awaited the guests – Jean Seberg and Anna Piaggi, the stylist Tan Giudicelli who had just left Chloé, Gaby Aghion and Paloma Picasso, Manolo Blahnik and Helmut Newton – all of whom were somewhat stunned by so much magnificence.

Such opulent interiors, with candlelit dinners and guests to match, were at odds with the situation the country was facing. In 1976, over one million people in France were out of work. The steel industry had collapsed in the north, and the economic crisis was at the forefront of everyone's mind. But Karl Lagerfeld continued to live apart, immersed in the world of the European courts, as painted by Menzel. "I have never made a bed in my life," he would declare. "What's more, I don't even carry a key." The truth is that he had never worked harder. But he promoted the dream he was living all over the place: "I should like to have lived at the court of Frederick the Great." Fittingly, the American press had found a nickname for him that matched his delusions of grandeur: *Kaiser...*

At about 9am on the morning of a Chloé catwalk show, Sonia Rykiel would always be the first on the phone to Karl, to ward off bad luck: "Shit!" She would present her own collection in the late afternoon and he would send her an armful of white flowers to bring her luck in return. Did his public find him unsympathetic? He was a very good friend to the designers he liked.

Karl loved Rykiel: a designer three years his senior, whose knitwear moulded so elegantly to the body of the working woman. She was extremely thin, funny, as disciplined as he was, adventurous and uncompromising. During one of her fashion shows, when she was still more widely known in France than he was, she dressed one of her models in shorts by Kenzo and a Chloé blouse that Karl had designed; she pinned his name onto the blouse in big letters, 'Lagerfeld', so that the photographers would see it.

Karl accompanied Sonia to Asia on a trip organised by the chamber of commerce for the fashion industry. He would often dine with her – and with Kenzo and Jacques, of course. Karl did not have all that many friends in the fashion world and Nathalie, Sonia's daughter, fancied Jako...

To celebrate Nathalie's twentieth birthday, Karl designed a magnificent silk dress for her, covered in handwritten messages: 'Long Live Nathalie', 'Long Live Love'. The dress arrived late, in a huge box with the Chloé logo on it. Lagerfeld had added a drawing and a typical little message: 'You can even wear it to sleep in...'

10

When he moved to 'Pozzo', the nickname he gave to his private residence in the Rue de l'Université, Karl Lagerfeld sold all the furniture and vases from the apartment in Place Saint-Sulpice; gone was the Art Deco paraphernalia that had served as a backdrop to the early days of his life with Jacques de Bascher. He almost always made a clean sweep between the different phases of his life. As a couple, he and Jacques were on a new trajectory. They still went to parties and dinners together in Paris, but their relationship had become clearer. Karl created and paid. Jacques contributed a lack of inhibition that was missing from Karl's uptight nature. The Kaiser and his fool.

On the huge, empty expanse of black carpet in Place Saint-Sulpice, Jacques had installed the Harley-Davidson that Lagerfeld had bought him. Lagerfeld had given this same model of motorbike to his nephew, Christel's son, but the young man had died in a road accident. Since then, Karl insisted that Jacques stop using his bike – and thus the wondrous machine landed right in the middle of the drawing room. The glittering chrome produced a hilarious effect, particularly when Jacques sat on the bike in just his leather trousers, looking dangerous and seductive. This was where he entertained his gang: a mixture of gay intelligentsia, thugs picked up on the street and large, demonstrative queens.

Karl was invited to participate in the celebrations for Kenzo's thirty-ninth birthday. The Japanese dress designer was so delightful that he appeared to have no enemies. Jacques was in charge of organising this party, and he invited his gang of riotous hedonists to join him for the preparations. The party was to be held on 11 March 1978, with the theme of 'Vice Versa': the boys were to dress as girls and the girls as boys. Each was to be called by the name of the parent of the opposite sex. Jako became 'Armelle', but his costume would certainly not have won Madame de Bascher's approval.

The six wardrobes in Place Saint-Sulpice that contained Jacques's impressive clothes collection were completely cleared out. Everyone dived in, searching for skirts and wigs; Jacques had as many fancy dress costumes as he had street clothes. Jacques/Armelle dressed as the inhabitant of a brothel: corset, suspenders and fish-net stockings. Kenzo and his partner, Xavier de Castella, went as gypsies: long legs and high heels. The others wore taffeta petticoats or gold lamé mini-skirts.

A whole bunch of them left the flat, dressed up, to get on a hired bus that was waiting in the square. The party was to take place in a new club that the proprietor of Le Sept, Fabrice Emaer, had opened ten days earlier at 8 Rue du Faubourg-Montmartre: Le Palace. "The Palace is first and foremost a theatre, it will allow people to be actors and spectators at the same time. The theatre is a free space, so the Palace is a place of liberty," Emaer proclaimed. As may be imagined, everyone immediately got the point. What an arrival! On the staircase leading to the basement, dozens of girls with very low voices giggled and swayed. Hairy chests exploded from corsets; Jacques wore his hair in big bunches like a teenager; Kenzo had electric blue eyeshadow on. "The star was Mick Jagger, wearing a blonde wig and blue satin miniskirt, with a Rolling Stones tee shirt on top," recalled Philippe Heurtault, who photographed the whole baroque parade. The model Jerry Hall was beside the singer of 'Sympathy for the Devil', wearing a dinner jacket with a narrow moustache painted on her top lip.

Karl never took part in these parties, or else he would leave very early. But he loved the detailed, lively accounts Jacques gave of them – as well as his accurate descriptions of the extravagant outfits, his keen eye for accessories and his brilliantly entertaining fund of gossip! Jako was Karl's look out for the world of the night – which was often the same as the world of fashion. Jako would probably have liked to play a larger part in Karl's success as a couturier. But what more could he do, this handsome young man who seemed to like nothing more than to amuse himself?

De Bascher had style and ideas. He maintained a long friendship with two painters he admired, David Hockney and Francis Bacon; he would have liked to buy a drawing or a painting by one of them but Karl was deaf to his entreaties and refused his request. Jacques lacked the organisation, the application and the courage to produce a film or a book himself. In 1977, to mark the launch of the Fendi prêt-à-porter collection, the Kaiser managed to persuade the Italian fashion house to commission Jacques to make a short film, the first of its kind, to promote the brand's aesthetic. The screenplay is by Jacques de Bascher, but it is full of references to Lagerfeld: a young American woman persuades her parents that she is taking the waters in Baden-Baden, the German spa town, when she is actually wandering around Rome, wearing clothes by Fendi. She also invents herself a cat called Karl, and if we did not see her in the nude, trying on furs designed by Lagerfeld, it would be difficult to see what Jacques's input had been. He chose the title, however, *Histoire d'eau,* a gently provocative reference to *Histoire d'O,* the erotic film by Just Jaeckin released two years earlier.

"The filming was infernal," Lagerfeld later told Marie Ottavi, Jacques's biographer. "Jacques began work at about 5 or 6pm. He slept all day. Then he would stop work early to join the Roman night life. I only ever saw him when he had gotten over his hangover." This was to be the last time Karl ever tried to introduce Jako to his working life. Even writing an article for one of the trendy magazines then flourishing in Paris seemed more than he could manage. Every time he would get started. Every time he would give up, overwhelmed by the effort. After the Roman experience, Karl preferred to just give him the money that Jacques seemed incapable of earning. He was carried away by the vice of indolence.

Karl was his exact opposite. He got up when his friend went to bed. Work was his pleasure. He outshone all the stylists who worked for Gabrielle Aghion at Chloé – to such an extent that they all threw in the towel and left him to fulfil the orders himself. He thus ruled over the fashion house single-handedly, making Chloé the most iconic brand of the 1970s. Collaborating with thirty or so other labels – clothes, underwear, shoes, accessories, decoration – he was without any doubt the most productive designer in Paris.

His capacity implies a matchless discipline. In Lagerfeld's studios, there was no shouting and no hysterical fits. Apart from his almost pathological tendency to be late – he usually arrived at appointments two or three hours after the appointed time – he had none of the foibles that usually manifested in the creatively gifted. What was more, he could design his collection, supervise the fittings and listen to the press communiqué being read out – all at the same time. Highly intelligent, he kept an eye on all the latest trends, took inspiration from what he saw, then absorbed and digested it, following the excellent synthetisation process Antonio Lopez taught him. He was always alert, always lying in wait. "During the collections, he would hire temporary designers who went from studio to studio," Anita Briey, then a dressmaker for Chloé, remembered. "He instantly knew what was going on in all the different fashion houses."

For sure, Karl didn't have many creations to his own name. No dinner jackets for women, no safari jackets; no Mondrian dress or retro fashion – all those inspired ideas that added up to the 'Saint Laurent style'. But most of Lagerfeld's clothes won commercial success, nevertheless: his 'Accent' skirt, soon after the minis of May 1968; his baby doll dresses, mink blousons, de-structured silk dresses and lace inserts, the latter inspired by Anna Piaggi's underwear; all of these made his fortune. Nevertheless, his acute awareness of the period made him realise that his image lacked the spice that would place him at the crazy Seventies' heart.

At Le Sept and the Palace, everyone was sleeping with everyone else. Everyone was taking drugs, too. Anyone trying to dry out had to escape, otherwise they would hit the habit again. Corey Tippin had said goodbye to Paris: "Too druggy," he said; "keeping pace with the rhythm of crazy, expensive parties – too much." It threatened to destroy him. He was not the only person trying to escape. "In 1975, I was twenty-six but I was already so seriously hooked on heroin that a friend recommended a drying-out clinic," Thierry Ardisson told me; he was a regular customer at Le Sept. "I went to Santa Barbara in California for three months. When I returned, it was to a completely different milieu." Others, like Jacques de Bascher, stumbled from one drug-induced high to the next.

"He would leave the house with a Coca-Cola bottle full of cocaine in his jacket pocket and would inhale the cocaine through a straw," Philippe Heurtault told me. Jacques needed more and more money to feed his cocaine habit. He drank impressive quantities of whisky and took a mixture of pills, alcohol and poppers. "There was a morbid, suicidal element in his make-up so that, in spite of his attractiveness, this was the impression you were left with," said Frédéric Mitterand, who frequented the same bars and the same parties at the time.

Karl Lagerfeld was never tempted. After a single glass of wine, he felt as if he was losing control. "I'm a Calvinist, attracted by superficiality," was his claim. With his mother, he had created a sort of super-ego. With Jacques, he experienced sexual urges and fantasies vicariously. "I do not have his appetite for all those things he takes," he said, "but it's catching." He could not have stated the situation more explicitly. "Lagerfeld and Saint Laurent each had their power behind the throne, who would live for them and report back on how things were going," explained Paquita Paquin, the Palace's head physiognomist at the time.

After the disastrous *Histoire d'eau*, Karl decided to let Jacques develop his talent at what he did best. He asked him to organise evening entertainments for him with more and more frequency. He ordered everything and paid, while his partner took on the wild and whacky planning.

For their first attempt, the Kaiser requested "something that will make an impression," and his assistant suggested a party so crazy that it is still remembered, even forty years later, with a shudder of fascination mixed with revulsion.

The party took place on the same evening as the Chloé catwalk show, during prêt-à-porter week. 'Karl Lagerfeld and Jacques de Bascher invite you, on 24 October 1977, to a party: Moratoire noir(e) [Black Moratorium]. Tragic black dress obligatory' – so says the invitation card, which was sent out to... four thousand people. Somewhere larger than the tiny dance floor at Le Sept had to be found, so Jako took the Rolls to Montreuil to visit La Main bleue (The Blue Hand): an old warehouse that had been redecorated by Philippe Starck, where, every evening, to the strains of funk and African music, all the '*sapeurs noirs*' (black francophone dandies from Africa) gathered from the Parisian suburbs.

As usual, Karl Lagerfeld paid for everything. Never mind the exorbitant cost. He always spent his money, never made any investments. "I detest rich people who live below their income," he said, in lordly fashion. Even before proceedings began, there was a whiff of scandal. It was said that the party had been organised in honour of Andreas Baader, the German terrorist from the Red Army Faction who had just committed suicide in prison. As if Lagerfeld, the elitist, and de Bascher, the monarchist, would pay homage to a far-left revolutionary extremist!

Was this why the couturier only made a brief appearance at the start of the party, wearing Dracula's black cape with a whitened face? Or was it because he had immediately taken stock of the direction in which the evening was moving? Jacques and Xavier de Castella – Kenzo's partner and a great friend of Jacques's – welcomed the guests in white fencing gear; during the run-up to the party they had painted the sleeves with fluorescent red paint from an aerosol. They were the only people not wearing the 'tragically black' mourning clothes stipulated in the invitation. Both arrived with their heads covered by black mantillas, in order not to be recognised. Jacques wore a devilish smile, while Xavier had on one of those sado-masochistic balaclavas with holes only for the eyes and mouth. Eros and Thanatos united.

"It was a party that we wouldn't have missed for the world," laughed Paquita Paquin, "but it wasn't until we read the papers the next day that we realised what had happened." On the stage, the writer Pierre Combescot had agreed to dance *Swan Lake,* dressed in a black tutu. David Pontremoli, a handsome blonde Franco-Italian actor with a back catalogue of mediocre appearances in films, sang '*Una lacrima sul viso*' while whipping the young man at his feet. The young Maria Schneider, who, several years earlier, had starred in the film *Last Tango in Paris* by Bernardo Bertolucci, paraded her brown curls amongst the overexcited guests. Everyone drank white wine produced on the De Bascher property in Brittany, La Berrière, which hugely augmented the effects of cocaine, heroin and Mandrax, as well as the smoke of the poppers. "It was a confusion of mourning clothes and boys in black leather," wrote Alain Pacadis the next-but-one day in *Libération*. "Wine flowed freely, and on the stage warriors from *Star Wars* fought with torches; there were scenes of fist-fucking and retro transvestites. Never in Paris have been seen so many guys in black leather gathered together in the same place."

None of this upset Lagerfeld. He had never wanted to conform to bourgeois morality. In spite of the scandal – at least half the guests left La Main bleue, appalled, in the middle of the party, and the Mayor of Montreuil wanted to close down this scene of debauchery permanently the following day – the story of the Moratoire noir(e) was soon the subject of every conversation. "It was undoubtedly one of the most successful parties of the year, that and the marriage of Loulou de la Falaise," was how Pacadis ended his article. At last, Karl had drawn level with the Saint Laurent clan. In fact, the party was just a foretaste of the period now beginning, as gay clubs opened and the culture spread. "Basically, Le Moratoire was the first backroom in Paris," remarked Paquita Paquin. Which was exactly what Karl wanted: to anticipate the current climate.

In 1975, André Leon Talley, the reporter from *Interview,* soon to become one of the editors of *American Vogue,* declared himself impressed by the pair – the couturier and the dandy – and asked if their way of life could be considered decadent. "In the USA, decadence has connotations of schlock, pornography, filth," Jacques replied. "*Décadence* in France is something quite different; it is a means of descending into beauty."

After Montreuil, the best parties were thrown at Le Palace. Guy Cuevas, former DJ of Le Nuage, ran the disco;

his collection of records had no rival in France, mixing funk, soul, Caribbean rhythms and sounds from Brazil. The Palace disco would shortly become the soundtrack to the 1970s. Cuevas had the idea of mixing 'La Vie en rose' for Grace Jones, thus propelling this sublime black singer to iconic status during the Palace's opening party. Ever since, Fabrice Emaer was on the look out for something new every evening to ensure that his nightclub kept its lead.

Was it the reputation of Le Moratoire that produced this effect? On 12 April 1978, the proprietor of the Palace asked Jacques to organise a masked ball. 'Angels and Devils' was to be the theme. These parties were an opportunity for all the different clans to get together. People could be enemies or rivals, but the world of fashion was so close-knit that everyone always went to the same places to dine and dance.

On the appointed day, a crowd of cherubs and devils thronged the entrance. Loulou de la Falaise sported red and gold wings designed by Saint Laurent, while her husband Thadée Klossowski was in white, an immaculate feather crown upon his head. Wearing a tall pointed hat and an ample black cape, Lagerfeld was disguised as Nostradamus, or perhaps Merlin the Wizard. Anna Piaggi was a Gorgon, François-Marie Banier a magician. The young Eva Ionesco – thirteen years old! – whose mother exhibited erotic photography in the Parisian galleries without anyone turning a hair, burst in as a naked elf. In the midst of all these fairies and little devils was Jacques, disguised as Icarus, wearing a headdress of blue, pink and mauve feathers.

He was burning up, for sure. But although Karl had banned the motorbike, he forbore from condemning self-destruction by late nights and cocaine. He found it very interesting, anyway. "These parties played host to crazy invention," commented the designer Vincent Darré. "We spent days and days combing the flea markets for costumes to wear. We dressed to impress the stylists, and sometimes our disguises could be found in their fashion shows."

In the long catalogue of parties that studded the period, worth mentioning is Fabrice Emaer's Venetian ball, financed by Lagerfeld on 25 October 1978. The party was one year after the Moratoire noir(e), and its exact opposite. "From the city of the Doges to the city of the gods," says the card, in the shape of a black lacquered wolf. The costumes were amazing. Above his velvet doublet, Jacques wore a headdress he had had fashioned out of plywood, measuring nearly three metres long, which represented the Rialto Bridge. A little cloth curtain allowed him to conceal or reveal his face. The ballet dancer Rudolf Nureyev came dressed as a white Pierrot. Anna Piaggi was a Venetian fisherwoman, with a dish of real seafood fixed to the top of her head; the seafood had to be thrown away during the evening as the heat made the molluscs go bad. Lagerfeld, as usual, was the least extraordinary. He kept his ponytail and fan, but adopted a tricorn hat and a long Renaissance robe, worn over white stockings and shoes.

To add spice to the evening, Fabrice Emaer arranged for Jenny Bel'Air, the most spectacular drag queen at the Palace, to arrive in a gondola at a high point of the evening, carried on the shoulders of a gang of porters. The boat had not gone ten metres when the gang tripped and fell – Jenny's skirt flew up, revealing all that lay beneath.

On 10 May 1981, most of the rich and beautiful in France voted for Giscard d'Estaing. François Mitterand's victory sent a chill over their extravagant festivities. The only subject of conversation round the tables of Le Privilège, the exclusive club opened by Fabrice Emaer to make up the gap in the Palace's finances, was tax. Guy and Marie-Hélène de Rothschild, whose parties were so popular, had already left for New York, and Helmut Newton had chosen tax exile in Monaco.

What about Lagerfeld? "I possess nothing, I just receive a percentage on everything," he used to say. In its 1981 investigation into the finances of prêt-à-porter designers, Women's Wear Daily (WWD) included him immediately in their ranking. "Rich, rich, rich, rich, rich, rich, rich" was the title of the article, and the figures were mind-blowing. Pierre Cardin, with his huge portfolio of licences, was richest (8 to 9 million dollars a year), but Hubert de Givenchy, Saint Laurent and Pierre Bergé weren't far behind (approximately 4 million dollars each). Lagerfeld came fifth. The WWD journalist calculated that he must be earning about 3.5 million dollars a year.

"You should come and join us on the Rock," Helmut Newton suggested. And so, three months after the Socialist victory, Lagerfeld became a resident of Monaco. From then on, he lived at the top of the Roccabella, a tower block in which he bought two apartments on the same landing, overlooking the Mediterranean. One was for Jacques, the other for him. Newton, who lived a bit further up the hill, bought himself a telescope "for watching Karl's flat." He claimed he had spotted dozens of celebrities going in and out.

11

The brothers Alain and Gérard Wertheimer are extremely secretive. They never give interviews. The few photographs of them in circulation are taken in passing. Even the people who bump into them on the racecourse or at catwalk shows at their fashion house – where they are always in the fourth row, slightly overhanging – only have very ordinary things to say about them. "They don't talk much, and the person who has the most contact with them must be their horse trainer," a close friend told me. Rumour has it that one day, when Chanel had organised an event in New York, one of the brothers forgot to bring his invitation. He was unable to join the guests, as no-one at the entrance could identify him. So, we must rely on Karl Lagerfeld's version of how he was recruited by Chanel.

"One day I received a phone call from Kitty d'Alessio…" It was 1982, and Chanel's New York director wanted to sound Lagerfeld out about his intentions. This elegant brunette had been keeping an eye on Lagerfeld for several years; she had admired his dresses and furs, worn only by the most elegant American women. Lagerfeld had invited her to dinner, as well as to his parties in both

New York and Paris, and his *savoir-faire*, his dazzling conversation and the wealth of his clientele had not escaped her notice. On the fortieth floor of the building at 9 West 57th Street – the Chanel headquarters – Kitty d'Alessio was well placed to appreciate, through the huge glass windows, the branches of the trees in Central Park – and, in the quiet, comfortable offices, her bosses' strategic interrogation.

Eight years earlier, Alain Wertheimer had taken over the family business, after persuading the board of directors to declare his father, Jacques, incompetent. Jacques Wertheimer, who lived in an apartment on Avenue Foch, surrounded by works of art and without a regret in the world, was soon thereafter placed under guardianship. At the age of thirty-four, the elder of the two Wertheimer brothers had already quietly re-structured the business, reintegrated the production and the distribution of the prêt-à-porter lines and returned the perfumes to their former glory (Chanel No. 5 was still the house's best-seller) by preventing their sale in drugstores. "This young man is effortlessly secretive," Alain Wertheimer's few close friends would say about him. "He is sincerely secretive. It is a matter of good manners to him, and by now almost a philosophy." Kitty d'Alessio was aware that he now planned to revamp the couture department and give the luxury business a global image. To accomplish this ambition, she thought of Lagerfeld.

How could the artistic director of Chloé and Fendi resist Chanel's allure? In Paris, a new generation of designers had arrived: Claude Montana, Thierry Mugler, Azzedine Alaïa. In addition, Japanese designers like Yohji Yamamoto and Rei Kawakubo, the founder of Comme des Garçons, were shaking up the fashion scene. Karl Lagerfeld's only real fear was of being superseded.

Chanel was an illustrious and ageing brand, but the Wertheimers were rich. Richer than Gabrielle Aghion, the creator of Chloé, and the Fendi sisters combined. Although Karl might swear by prêt-à-porter to everyone, Chanel was a fashion house that had retained its haute couture workshops. To join them would be to enter at last the great portals of the design elite who, in his mind, continued to give him the cold shoulder.

Above all, Lagerfeld knew what the house in Rue Cambon represented for Saint Laurent, his eternal rival. In 1968, in reply to Proust's question, "Who are your heroines in history?", the prince of fashion had replied without hesitation: "Gabrielle Chanel." In that same year, the 'Grande Mademoiselle' singled him out as her spiritual successor. When Coco died in her suite at the Ritz Hotel, in 1971, it was Yves who was stopped by the photographers of the world, coming down the steps of the Madeleine after her funeral. If Karl became Chanel's successor – so he thought, with secret satisfaction – this was a revenge the Saint Laurent-Bergé duo would simply have to put up with.

At the beginning of the 1980s, however, Chanel's products were far out of fashion. In France, only Simone Veil, Marie-France Garaud and the wife of the aeroplane manufacturer Marcel Dassault were left to pose for the magazines in the famous braided coat and skirt. The success of the perfumes never faltered, but now that a socialist president had succeeded to the Élysée Palace, haute couture smacked of the years of Pompidou and Giscard: a bygone age.

Clients still came to the hallowed salons of Rue Cambon for fittings. In 1973, when Marie-Louise de Clermont-Tonnerre joined to run the press office, she was struck by the atmosphere – like a sanctuary. "When my friends asked me what effect it had had on me to move from Cardin to Chanel, I would answer: 'I have the impression of joining a Protestant bank…'" The two heads of the workshop, 'Monsieur Jean' and 'Madame Yvonne', ruled sternly over the couture seamstresses, but although Philippe Guibourgé, a stalwart from Dior, had launched the prêt-à-porter, no-one had yet managed to revitalise Chanel's style.

It was the same abroad. "A year before Karl arrived, I wrote an article for *Stern* [the German magazine], photographed by Peter Lindbergh: 'The ten classics of fashion', the trench coat, the white shirt" – so I was told by Florentine Pabst, Lagerfeld's German friend. "When I suggested the Chanel coat and skirt, Lindbergh replied: 'Does that old thing still survive?'"

Kitty d'Alessio had observed the success and fame enjoyed by Lagerfeld, who everyone now nicknamed the Kaiser. Having previously worked in publishing, she was able to gauge better than anyone the growing importance of 'branding' in selling a product. With his 'looks', his culture, his work as a stylist for Chloé and Fendi, and his many collaborations in Europe and Japan, Lagerfeld was the only person (apart from Saint Laurent) who had a reputation abroad. He was forty-nine, and now was the time to change.

"I met Alain Wertheimer in his house in London and we talked for a long time," Karl Lagerfeld remembered. "I saw the way Gabrielle Chanel, at the end of her life, suddenly cut herself off from her period by criticising jeans and mini-skirts, which the youth of the whole world now wanted to wear. It was as if she had signed her death warrant. But I knew her world very well…"

This is probably what reassured Alain Wertheimer from the outset. To choose a German to personify a brand that was so quintessentially French was daring. "He knows more about Chanel than I do," the owner of the fashion house confided to his friends. And Karl, of course, used all his charm and knowledge to his advantage. "At the end of the discussion," Karl claimed, "he said to me: 'Do what you like, but if it doesn't work, I'm selling!' I replied: 'Write that into the contract, *Do what you like*.'"

The communiqué that Chanel sent out on 15 September 1982 is carefully worded and vague: 'From January 1983, the life and the imagination of Chanel's haute couture collection will benefit from the artistic direction of Karl Lagerfeld.' The financial conditions outlined in the contract look exceptional: a million dollars for two couture collections per year, and the Chanel prêt-à-porter

– this was the figure guessed at by *Women's Wear Daily*, the American bible of the fashion trade.

Lagerfeld also negotiated 100,000 dollars' worth of clothes for the 'editors of the fashion press and for friends.' He knew the importance of taking care of people who would show off his clothes in the media and at social events, and now his genius for communication was recognised. "I only like working for big companies who have plenty of advertising clout," he told *WWD*, the week before his first haute couture collection. He clearly intended to give maximum visibility to this collaboration, throughout the world.

As usual, Karl left nothing to chance. Some months earlier, he had rented a huge apartment in Rue de Rivoli, a couple of blocks from Rue de Cambon, for his assistant Hervé Léger. Hervé was officially taken on to look after the prêt-à-porter until Lagerfeld's exclusive contract with Chloé came to an end in December 1983. Then Lagerfeld dug into the archives.

He did not just want to learn Coco's story – that, he already knew. He knew she had re-invented her past – an adventurous father who went to make his fortune in New York – to hide the fact that she was an orphan sent as a maid-of-all-work to farming families. He had read endlessly about her myth-making and her lies. Alain Wertheimer's mother, Éliane, told him how, during the occupation, she had appealed to the German authorities to return the ownership of Chanel perfumes to her "because it is now the property of Jews." While she made this shameless imploration, the Wertheimers had to emigrate to the USA to escape the Nazis.

Éliane Heilbronn was a lawyer. Her divorce from Jacques Wertheimer, Alain and Gérard's father, followed by her remarriage, did not distance her from the fashion house; she continued to provide her sons with legal advice, including the supervision of Karl's mouth-watering contract. Karl attracted her immediately, with his culture and wit. She understood his desire to know everything about Gabrielle Chanel, including the less savoury aspects, and often told him stories that were not in the books: memories retained by the Wertheimers of this couturière whom they continued to finance, even after she tried to rob them.

What Karl was primarily looking for, however, was the essence of the style. The DNA of the brand. Chanel was a weighty heritage to take on. All over the world, people were still wearing her coats and skirts or – the ultimate accolade – copies of her trousers with the double-buttoned fly, worn with a striped tee shirt. Marilyn's husky voice, whispering that she only wore a spritz of Chanel No. 5 to sleep in, lent the name an erotic aura – but the house was best known for the classics, which Karl now had to re-invent.

As anticipated, the announcement of his arrival at Chanel caused widespread shock in the fashion world. Saint Laurent, of course, whose addiction to drugs and alcohol did not affect his talent (but whose periods of depression, which left him looking haggard for days on end, were well known) took the news like a 'stab in the back' – so his clan soon realised. Pierre Bergé also had to revoke his disdainful comments about Karl, now that the latter was moving into haute couture. Karl's arrival also affected Chanel's traditional clients, many of whom had known the Grande Mademoiselle personally. And finally, Gabrielle Aghion was shaken. To lose Karl Lagerfeld was to lose the person who had set Chloé off on the road to success. On the day of the final catwalk show at Chloé, all the seamstresses were in tears. A huge piece of canvas had been stretched out below the podium. Someone had painted a small aeroplane on the canvas, piloted by an aviator with a ponytail, taking off towards the skies.

The couturier was keenly awaited in the Chanel camp. To give Karl Lagerfeld the freedom he requested, Alain Wertheimer had taken pains to dismiss anyone who might hold him back. Philippe Guibourgé, the head of prêt-à-porter, had not had his contract renewed. 'Monsieur Jean' and 'Madame Yvonne' had been encouraged to retire. The press office was strengthened. Only Jacques Helleu, the elegant artistic director of perfumes and watches, managed to preserve his territory. With his culture, his aesthetic awareness and his sense for marketing, he was one of the few employees who might be a match for Karl. Thanks to him, Helmut Newton and Richard Avedon had been involved in his best advertising campaigns, and Catherine Deneuve had become the doyenne of perfumes. Wertheimer was not prepared to take the risk of dislodging him. "Helleu was powerful, and Chanel No. 5 was still the fashion house's biggest earner," said Jacques Polge, who joined Chanel in 1978 and was, at the time, preparing the launch of Coco: the latest 'juice'. "Then we moved to Neuilly, which might as well have been the provinces for the people in Rue Cambon…"

At last, the day arrived: 25 January 1983. Isabelle Adjani was among the first to arrive in Rue Cambon, her blue eyes hidden behind dark glasses. The actor Jean-Claude Brialy followed, along with Paloma Picasso and the perfumer Hélène Rochas. The d'Ormessons, Claude Pompidou and the baroness Marie-Hélène de Rothschild, all faithful admirers of Gabrielle Chanel, led the small troop of clients. A crowd of fashion editors came in from America and Europe.

Karl Lagerfeld was well aware that this was a watershed. Could a designer of prêt-à-porter breathe new life into haute couture? Could a man replace one of the few women to have gained celebrity in this world? Could a German embody the very essence of French fashion? These were the questions that had been circulating, in the months since his appointment.

To silence the comments about his nationality, Karl planned to open his first fashion show with three models, one in a blue coat and skirt, the second in a white one, the third in a red one, accompanied by the songs of Édith Piaf and Charles Trenet. *"Douce France, cher pays de mon enfance..."* The skirts were a bit shorter, just below the knee, the shoulders more structured, and the signature Chanel cravat was replaced by a scarf knotted below a pearl necklace. "I kept Chanel's spirit, but I gave it a little up-to-date twist," Karl Lagerfeld explained on television. In a pinstripe suit like a banker, wearing huge aviator's glasses, he seemed somewhat ill-at-ease in a style he had not yet had time to digest.

The press reaction was mixed on the following day. 'Is it by him, or is it by her? Each garment raises the same question,' wrote Janie Samet in *Le Figaro*. 'Kaiser Karl is responsible for too much Chanel not to imitate her, and not enough Chanel to imitate her,' *Women's Wear Daily* complained, adding that 'Lagerfeld is marking time. No-one can replace Chanel, not even Kaiser Karl, and no-one should try to do so.' The report by the television news on Antenne 2 was no more friendly: "Henceforward, the height of the 'look' will be to wear fake Chanel made in the actual workshops of Maison Chanel," was the journalist's sour addition.

"He has a good feeling for Chanel, but he hasn't yet made it," remarked Marie-Hélène de Rothschild, one of Chanel's most faithful customers, who had previously been dressed by Coco herself. Quoted in *WWD*, she explains: "Someone needs to tell him a bit more about her. Her proportions were so perfect… But no-one could achieve that at the first attempt. It will come." This was Lagerfeld's problem in a nutshell: people wanted a repeat and a change at the same time.

We need to consider this challenge, before we move on. This was, in fact, an area in which Lagerfeld excelled, considering how much he enjoyed 'exercises in style': his method of applying modern touches to a classic pattern. He was a chameleon. Balmain, Patou, Chloé and Fendi – each time, he had wormed his way into a fashion house that was not his own and managed to sublimate its spirit. After so many years spent reading, collecting images and feeding on photographs and paintings, he had retained the DNA of each of his colleagues. Here was a man who – it was reported – had the entire history of fashion since the 1920s in his head.

Ralph Toledano, the current president of the chamber of commerce of haute couture and formerly the director general of Maison Karl Lagerfeld, clearly remembers the evening before Gianfranco Ferré's first catwalk show for Dior, in 1989. Everyone was wondering: 'What will Ferré do?' According to Toledano, "Karl took his felt-tip pens and his pastels and began drawing. He sketched all the suits, the dresses and evening dresses, all Ferré's collection for Dior." He did not stop there: "Someone else asked him: 'And Saint Laurent?' And he had done the same. 'And Sonia Rykiel?' The same. Everything was perfectly 'in the manner of…'"

After his first low-key fashion show, Karl returned to the Chanel archives and systematically drew up a catalogue of Coco's most iconic inventions. Then he introduced that whiff of subversion that people expected. At the Palace, he had seen gorgeous girls dancing in Chanel's famous braided jacket, picked up at the flea market and shortened to the length of a blouson. As usual, Karl used his memories as an elixir to inspire him. He mixed day with night, expensive with inexpensive. The same tweed jacket, certainly – but shortened and worn with jeans. The famous camellia that Gabrielle loved so much, yes – but reproduced in celluloid as a brooch! He opted for short skirts and went wild with chains. The straw boater, the pearl encircled in gold, the black satin bow, the quilted handbag with a chain, it was all there – but transformed. He had never been shy of such anachronisms. At Chloé, he had already made his models parade in evening dress, worn with white plimsolls. Soon, he had Claudia Schiffer walking the catwalk in a bikini signed with two 'C's interlaced.

As usual, Karl resumed his press strategy with a phrase from Goethe, discovered in his parents' library of leather-bound books: 'You have to make a better future using elements from the past.' And it worked. "Karl is going to teach us about fashion," said Alain Wertheimer to Jacques Polge, Chanel's director of perfume. Chanel's owner had a sixth sense: sales rocketed from 1984.

In the workroom, the seamstresses immediately fell in love with Lagerfeld. These women – and a few men – were highly skilled and quick to spot the arrogance of the non-expert. It did not take Karl long to convince them that he was a master of the trade. Gabrielle Chanel had been a prize bitch: cantankerous and tough with the seamstresses. You only had to see her smoking, as she cut the three metres of fabric needed to make a coat and skirt directly on the tailor's dummy.

Her successor's sketches were accurate, clearly showing where to make cuts, the length of the back, the detail of a sleeve. When Karl came in for fittings, he always invited the head seamstress – 'Madame' Jacqueline, Olivia, Cécile or Josette – to sit down and give her opinion. He loved the way these women powdered their hands before they sewed; he loved their regional accents, the specialised vocabulary of the couture workshop and the ritual of concealing a hair in the hem of each wedding dress. Every 25 November, Karl Lagerfeld made it his business to design hats for the 'Catherinettes' [the unmarried seamstresses under the age of 25, who attended a yearly ball] *according to their taste and personality. He had these hats made by Pierre Debard, hat maker to Michel, the most prominent milliner in Paris.*

As soon as he arrived, he was delighted to discover Madame Pouzieux, a farmer from Montargis who, since 1947, had been weaving braid and haberdashery for Chanel in a workshop beside her barn. At last, he had found what he was missing: the combination of a craft industry and financial power.

12

Shortly after his arrival in Rue Cambon, Karl Lagerfeld had an advertising brainwave. Gabrielle Chanel was the only woman to have made her name in fashion. The only one, too, whose short haircut and elegant, boyish appearance could be recognised even by a novice. Tall, dark haired and very slender, Inès de la Fressange had something of the look of 'Coco'.

Karl had already bumped into this beautiful girl at the Palace, and had seen her in Oliviero Toscani and Paolo Roversi's photographs, which had made her a star on a number of magazine covers. He had never yet booked her for a Chloé fashion show. With her overly long arms and her untypical, extremely slender body, she did not fit ready-made clothing, where nothing is tailored to measure. Things were different in haute couture though, and since she had become a big hit, Karl began to take an interest in this young woman, whose pedigree so delighted Jacques de Bascher. "Karl would always wait to see if you were successful before he selected you, then he would pretend to have launched you himself," Inès said recently, with a smile.

Whatever the story, it was Inès who, in the first catwalk show of January 1983, wore the evening dress that had the most commercial success. Some months later, Lagerfeld convinced her to sign an exclusive contract with Chanel, unheard of in the world of couture. She became both the image and the style of the house, the reincarnation of 'Mademoiselle'. She wore many more garments than the other models in the show: twenty changes instead of the usual five. She also had to wear Chanel whenever she was seen in public. She and Lagerfeld got on so well that "when we went on tour, the hoteliers used to make me inspect Karl's suite as if I was Madame Lagerfeld," she laughed.

Physically, this twenty-five-year-old woman was six feet tall and weighed less than nine stone – perfect for Chanel's coats and skirts: "Fine build, no bust, narrow hips, so the jacket hangs perfectly," was the comment of one of the seamstresses in the couture workshop. "The boyish look in a woman is very inspiring," said Lagerfeld; he began to design his collections with Inès in mind. The couturier loved her cheeky expressions, as well as her excellent education.

'La Fressange', as he sometimes called her, had just the right amount of irreverence, combined with that 'aristocratic' chic that amused him so much. Lagerfeld allowed her to 'perform' on the catwalk: she took extra-long strides, swung her arms, blew kisses and sometimes even smoked. "Move as if you were wearing jeans," the designer would say.

He introduced denim into his collections in 1984. And trainers. In short, after his first low-key show, Lagerfeld decided to "make Chanel turn in her grave", proclaiming that "At least that will show that she is still alive!" To conservatives who balked at denim, he made the following retort on the news: "We need to keep the idea of Chanel, but for today's woman. We are not here to clothe people obsessed with the past, or grannies – they don't count in fashion."

Gabrielle had installed herself at the top of the famous staircase at Rue Cambon, where several mirrors stood that had been arranged to blur fiction with reality. The door to the studio lay along many winding corridors. During the '80s, Karl had it decorated by Andrée Putman in shades of grey, black and white. Although the word '*Mademoiselle*' was still written on the door, the atmosphere was radically changed. When the older generation retired, a new team was put in place: self-educated, daughters of friends, friends of friends – the faithful, in a word. "I want beautiful young people around me," Karl insisted.

Inès de la Fressange brought her own gaiety and sparkle, making suggestions that no other model would dare to risk. "It was the merriest studio and the least pretentious in Paris," she remembers. "Anything might become a new idea. I drew my dog? 'We'll make it into a button,' Karl ordered. I described a sea-green outfit spotted in a painting by the artist Watteau? The next day he had designed a little taffeta trouser suit in the same colour."

Gilles Dufour was director of the studio, a designer who had worked with Lagerfeld at Chloé. He was a good-looking, talented young man who had been introduced to the jet-set; he was often seen in Rudolf Nureyev's company. He despised anything to do with intrigue or rivalry. His niece, Victoire de Castellane, was in charge of jewellery at Chanel. She was the great-granddaughter of Boni de Castellane, the celebrated Belle Époque dandy. Witty and imaginative, she might wear a little corset bought in Pigalle one day, with a tulle skirt worn like a ballet dancer's tutu; then a red suit and a skull cap with Mickey Mouse ears the next – which were later borrowed by Lagerfeld for the catwalk. Karl's assistant, Eric Wright, was a big black American who couldn't draw and didn't speak a word of French, but was unrivalled in his ability to match an accessory to a dress; he made everyone laugh with his cries of 'Fantastic!' when Lagerfeld so much as raised his little finger.

Visiting the studio became obligatory. 'The magic studio', the employees called it. Young Virginie Viard, who was later to succeed Karl, came as a design intern and could not bear to think of leaving. The American film director Francis Ford Coppola asked the actress Carole Bouquet if she could recommend his daughter – which is how Sophia Coppola, at the age of fifteen, accompanied by a female bodyguard who looked like a model, came to work among the sketches and scraps of fabric. "Karl wanted to be surrounded by amusing, good-looking people who were creative and unpretentious. In the end, we were more successful than Saint Laurent," said Gilles Dufour. In the evening, it was not unusual to see girls arriving at the Palace in mini-skirts, wearing a sleeveless top under a Chanel jacket that had been shortened and covered in paste beads. "It's simple enough," Victoire de Castellane told me: "we were a desirable fashion house."

The Wertheimers showed remarkable confidence. They only came to Paris from New York, where Alain lived, or from Geneva, where Gérard lived, for important meetings about the collections. "We were under no pressure from shareholders; we could spend money without accounting for it," Gilles Dufour still remembers. *'Karl'*, *'Karl'*, *'Karl'* – his first name, pronounced with reverence – became the 'open Sesame' to any adventure. *'Karl'* always flew to New York with Concorde, and travelled around Europe by private plane. A single accessory might be produced in ten different colours so that *'Karl'* could choose the one that went best with the gown he was designing. It all cost a fortune, but success had come so rapidly after his arrival that the proprietors gave *'Karl'* carte blanche.

Massaro the bootmaker, Lesage the embroiderer and Desrues, who made trimmings, all survived thanks to haute couture; in fact, these artisans were weighed down with orders. Lagerfeld designed rapidly and prolifically, and had the unrivalled ability to suggest twenty variations on a single detail. One day, one of the Wertheimer brothers challenged him to design an accessory inspired by an advertisement for a washing machine he had cut out of a magazine. "He took up the gauntlet," Martine Cartegini told me, who used to work at Chanel. "He based his design on the round window at the front of the washing machine and devised a series of tweed buttons covered in plexiglass!"

At the head of the press department, now employing about thirty people in France alone, Marie-Louise de Clermont-Tonnerre was swamped by the huge number of requests for interviews. Karl Lagerfeld was not only a creative dress-designer, he was also an exceptional communicator. He never regarded himself as an artist, however. "Making clothes is important, but they are only clothes," he would say. "I'm not Kierkegaard, all the same!" He was more interested in success than in posterity. "You have to ask yourself why people like it," he would continuously repeat to his disciples in the 'magic studio'. "Be an opportunist to the end."

He organised dinner parties for journalists at his house – sometimes two parties at once – sending a personal letter to each guest, accompanied by a huge bouquet of flowers. Inès de la Fressange also helped arrange VIP dinners in Paris or, when Karl was on tour, abroad. Fashion editors were showered with gifts, according to a power-based hierarchy: the editor-in-chief of American *Vogue*, Diana Vreeland (followed by Anna Wintour) was permitted to choose dresses, coats and skirts. Handbags, perfume and make-up were for the rest. To 'make women envious', he dressed prominent young women who might nowadays be referred to as 'influencers'.

Karl also groomed André Leon Talley, Vreeland and Wintours' closest collaborator at *Vogue*. André joined the magazine just as Lagerfeld was launching his first Chanel collection. With his height and his perfect French – modified by an American accent – ALT (as he was known) was a powerful figure. Black, the grandson of a domestic servant who had raised him, and a former pillar of Studio 54, the trendy New York discothèque of the 1970s, ALT had an unusual fashion career.

He was entertaining and cultivated, the prince of extravagance and the king of intrigue; it was he who, when he started work at Andy Warhol's magazine *Interview*, carried out the iconoclastic interviews with Karl and Jacques de Bascher. With a well-placed observation and a gesture that caricatured his subjects, he often set the tone for the fashion critics. He was a frequent guest at Grand-Champ and Pozzo, where he sat and wrote up pages to be devoted to Chanel in the forthcoming issue of *Vogue*, according to the amount of advertising Chanel had bought; the former always depended on the latter.

Lagerfeld also invited the journalists to accessorising sessions. Seated around him in the studio, a dozen or so hand-picked fashion editors would peruse the garments on the day before the catwalk show. Lagerfeld would choose the handbag, jewels and shoes and pretend to consult their opinion: "It's chic, isn't it?" If anyone dared say "Oh no, not that scarf!" he would remove it. "Make no mistake," someone familiar with the house added, "the scarf chosen by him would always re-appear on the catwalk."

Gabrielle Chanel had already been dressing actresses like Jeanne Moreau and Romy Schneider. Now a special salon for fittings was reserved for 'people', a word enjoying great success in France during the 1980s, which described celebrities who could sell products with far greater success than any advertising. Fashionable young women and beautiful singers were given bags and jewellery, which they would wear for the first time when they appeared on television.

Since he started living in Monaco for several months of the year, Karl had gotten to know the family of Prince Rainier – in particular his eldest daughter Caroline, who was endlessly pursued by the paparazzi after the death of her mother Grace in a car accident a year before. He had already met her when she was sixteen, during a 1973 photo session at his apartment in Place Saint-Sulpice. When *Vogue* invited the princess to be editor-in-chief of their Christmas issue, she chose Karl as her super-assistant. "We left at dawn to take some photographs at the Polo Club [in the Bagatelle], in my ancient Autobianchi," she remembered. "We had to break in and we laughed a lot; we became friends. He was so original, and so amazingly cultivated, that he could not fail to please right from the word go."

Like him, Caroline spoke several languages and lived in a world that resembled a backdrop. "I am not a muse, but I hope I amuse him," she declared, modestly. She did far more than that. When he first got to know her, he was impressed by her class, her history and her celebrity, but she later became a close friend. Karl introduced her to German literature – Eduard von Keyserling, his favourite, but also to Elizabeth von Arnim, an Englishwoman who lived in Berlin after her marriage to a Prussian count. With Karl, Caroline travelled from Paris to Luxor, "to contemplate two obelisks on the same day," as she put it. In the evening, they would go out with Jacques and Princess Stéphanie – "their two enfants terribles", said Karl – or would meet in one of the two apartments in Roccabella. Karl's apartment was designed for entertaining, decorated in the style of the Memphis Group – which, having been established in 1981, demonstrated the very latest in Italian design. There was a boxing ring in the middle of the salon.

"An interior is the natural projection of a soul," Paul Morand used to say. Which of Lagerfeld's interiors reflected his soul? His private residence in Paris: 1,500 square metres on the Rue de l'Université, all gilt, chandeliers with pendants and eighteenth-century mouldings, where he could sometimes be found in the kitchen, eating sausages dipped in Amora sauce? Or this ultra-contemporary flat, with its glimpse of the sea through a forest of concrete buildings?

Lagerfeld had acquired new notoriety and a powerful aura. In 1984 he took over the prêt-à-porter at Chanel, in addition to the haute couture. The following year, when his contract was renewed, he asked the proprietors to pay him a million dollars… for each collection. As if to show off his new power, Karl Lagerfeld signed a contract with the American manufacturer Bidermann Industries in 1983 to create prêt-à-porter and sportswear collections under his own name. Bidermann wanted to make him "the French Ralph Lauren". Lagerfeld, who "never wanted to put his name on a shop front", finally succumbed to this minor vanity project with its huge royalties.

He also managed to hold on to Fendi: in itself a little fashion revolution. The Wertheimers, whose house was so exclusive in every other respect, could find nothing to say against it. Since Lagerfeld's arrival, Chanel had been talked of throughout the world as never before. In August 1986, he received the Dé d'or (Golden Dice) for the best haute couture collection. "I am the first person to have made a name for myself with a name that is not my own," he joked.

From then on, Karl Lagerfeld designed eight collections a year: two haute couture and two prêt-à-porter collections for Chanel, two prêt-à-porter collections for Fendi and finally two collections in his own name. At night he slept only five or six hours, before spending the morning designing. After that, he would have to be tracked all afternoon to find out which fashion house he was visiting. Brahim, his driver, warned people when he was coming so they could fetch him the iced Pepsi and Coca-Cola that he drank all day. In the evening, Lagerfeld would organise press receptions. "I've seen Karl organise two or three dinner parties in order to entertain as many journalists as possible," Ralph Toledano assured me; Toledano had taken over as president of KL. The Kaiser was extending his empire every day. At last, the hour of vengeance had come.

Lagerfeld used to say "You need to move house regularly and always sell your old furniture," as if he were giving advice for a healthy lifestyle. He had found a new muse in Inès de la Fressange and, as usual, had discarded his old favourites. He broke with Anna Piaggi as one might throw out an old wardrobe: roughly and without a backward glance. The clashing combinations of 'couture' clothes from past seasons and second-hand items made Piaggi's outfits seem very 'seventies'; Karl declared them to be out of fashion and not at all in the spirit of Chanel. Make way for the charming BCBG (bon chic, bon genre) style of de la Fressange, far better adapted to the sparkling eighties.

Fabrice Emaer's death from cancer in 1983, followed by the death of Alain Pacadis, the chronicler of Karl's crazy parties, was the final nail in the coffin of the 1970s. Karl threw away that part of his past as a clod of earth is thrown into a grave. He broke permanently with any friends who were still linked to Saint Laurent; there was no question of being seen with Anne-Marie Muñoz, who had made Karl godfather to her son.

He made a clean sweep at Chanel, too. The couturier organised the dismissal of Kitty d'Alessio, who had introduced him to Alain Wertheimer. "It's her or me," he decreed, threatening not to appear on the catwalk at the end of one of the prêt-à-porter shows. Alain Wertheimer put up no resistance. "Between you and me, it's like being between Dr Faust and the devil," the Kaiser used to say. He ruled alone, from then on, in the house of others.

13

Most of his collaborators knew, though Karl Lagerfeld had told no-one. It wasn't difficult to see that Jacques de Bascher was no longer the flamboyant young man who used to dance so frenetically at the Palace. Since the mid-eighties he seemed to have declined a little more every day.

The frenzied, unbridled parties which fuelled his world were no longer fashionable. He was not working. When the painter Francis Bacon was in Paris, Jacques used to spend long afternoons drinking with him in his studio. "I'm in the midst of all his canvases – because you won't buy me one!" he would accuse Karl. He began mixing with shady types, making cynical, xenophobic remarks and flirting openly with the extreme Right.

Time after time, the couturier's colleagues saw him arrive drunk at mid-afternoon to ask for money, either at Chanel, or Avenue des Champs-Élysées, where the fashion label 'KL' had its studio. His mentor always gave him a handful of notes. Karl continued to support Jacques – though he no longer knew whether to encourage such an indolent life, or Jacques's dependence on alcohol and drugs.

Jacques would have liked to retain the use of his apartment in Place Saint-Sulpice, but since Saint Laurent had opened a prêt-à-porter boutique downstairs, Lagerfeld refused to let him keep it. Jacques lodged henceforward at Rue de Rivoli, in the huge apartment which looked out on the Tuileries – but the name *De Bascher* did not so much as appear on the letter-box. When he was in good shape, he visited the Chanel studio, only a few yards away. Otherwise he was prohibited from entering, and he was aware enough of social niceties not to approach Rue Cambon when he was high.

A few years earlier, he seemed to have found an escape from his unrealistic way of life. Diane de Beauvau-Craon, the crazy girl he used to meet at Le Sept during its glory days, returned to Paris in 1980, after a failed marriage in New York and a second union in Morocco – which had also been catastrophic, but from which she had gained a baby boy. "We reconnected as if we had said goodbye only yesterday, but this time, I got on better with Karl, because he realised that I did not have the same destructive, morbid nature that scared him in Jacques," she told me. How could Jacques, Diane and even Karl have dreamed up the engagement the De Bascher-Beauvau-Craon couple announced one evening in 1981?

Nevertheless, Jacques insisted that he was in love with this young, husky-voiced woman – with whom he posed as a chic pirate, wearing a black silk bandage over his eye, in the most celebrated photograph of the couple, which was taken one evening at the Opéra de Paris. The fact that she belonged to one of the most illustrious French families was clearly important to him, who used to pore over *L'Intermédiaire des chercheurs et curieux* every month, with its court and social news. He already spoke of having children.

Jacques and Diane had certain things in common. While both of them ricocheted between social life and drunken orgies, one was overtly gay, while the other was twice divorced. Their engagement surprised all their friends. Karl Lagerfeld welcomed the news. "Every day, Jacques continued to spend time with Karl, bringing him the latest rumours, and he knew this would continue," Diane assured me. "He loved Jacques, and valued him, providing him with the luxurious life he aspired to; but he was possessive, he wasn't jealous." Lagerfeld offered to host the dinner dance at which the couple would announce their future marriage. He paid for the cashmere jacket and white Bermuda shorts that Jacques wore for the evening, giving him the simultaneous appearance of a small boy out for a good time, and a tiger hunter. "He also chose the engagement ring, a truly sublime jewel," Diane de Beauvau-Craon continued. "It was not a game and he knew it, even though I did not take marriage very seriously."

As the descendant of one of the Colonna princesses, Diane had the right to an engagement ceremony in Rome, presided over by a cardinal; Jacques was thrilled. Once again, Karl drew out his wallet, financing the trip to Italy. The Fendi sisters loved the idea of this engagement, having known Jacques since he first met Lagerfeld; they took it upon themselves to organise the religious ceremony in the Spanish church of the Santissima Trinità, which they filled completely with flowers. Karl invited everyone to stay at Hotel Hassler. The decorator Andrée Putman and the actor Helmut Berger were to be witnesses, and the whole ceremony would be the height of elegance. The only problem was that the engaged couple refused to comply.

"We were terrible at that time," Diane told me. "The evening before the ceremony we had dinner with the Fendi sisters, who were so charming – then, when Karl had left so that we could rest before the big day, Jacques and I went out into the low dives of Rome…" The following day, did the cardinal notice the hollow eyes of the couple he was supposed to bless, before celebrating mass? "I hadn't enough saliva to take communion…" laughed Diane. But at last, this elegantly debauched duo were engaged.

What did Karl Lagerfeld expect of this union? Not that Jacques would become sensible: Diane de Beauvau was far from a demure young woman. But with her, Jacques was less gloomy, less destructive and perhaps more balanced; the couple went dancing every evening in a drug-fuelled trance. "And then, in the space of a year, Jako's behaviour changed. He wanted to continue going out, but to leave me shut up in the house like a housewife," said Diane, mixing English with French in her aristocratic way. "So I broke off the engagement. I think Karl was the most upset. Jako's fragile equilibrium had just been completely shattered."

After that, Jacques had more spare time than ever. He had been talking for years about making a film about Gilles de Rais, the medieval hero whose nineteenth-century portraits (depicting him as the wife-killing fairy-tale villain, Bluebeard) he collected. He loved Huysman's portrayal of this murderer of women and children as a decadent aesthete in *Là-bas*. Karl Lagerfeld refused to produce the film, however. Was Jacques equipped to move away from him, living as he did from hand to mouth when the pocket money from his mentor arrived even a fortnight late?

There was also a more serious matter. Since 1987, Jacques had been suffering from AIDS, the syndrome that had been ravaging the guests of those carefree seventies parties for the past five years. Driven by an instinct for self-preservation – unusual for him, a man who laughed at danger, stacking up the lovers of a previous evening like kills in an imaginary hunting log-book – he discreetly had himself tested for HIV. He continued his amorous career until the very last moment, brushing aside any possible threat. But by now he was visibly dwindling, and had become the victim of frequent infections which left him knocked out for weeks. Patrick Hourcade saw him at a catwalk show and was horrified. When he helped him on with his overcoat, "my hand slipped and I felt the sharp edge of his collarbone. He was horrifyingly thin." In Monaco, where Jacques de Bascher now lived for part of the year, he spent long hours wrapped up warmly on the terrace at 'La Vigie': a stunning white villa Karl rented by the Mediterranean, which looked like an Italian palace.

He was in his element in Paris, at parties every evening. In Monaco, where money dazzled wherever you looked, he seemed less comfortable, but that was exactly what he was looking for. He wanted to quit his aimless, disjointed life. Stalked by death, he didn't want his friends to see him. One Christmas Eve, the family of Prince Rainier – Caroline, Stéphanie and Albert – met him and Karl at midnight mass. "Jacques brought the Infant Jesus from his crib to have him blessed," Caroline remembers. He was nearly thirty-seven, and knew that he was dying.

After the arrival of AIDS, those in the worlds of fashion and night-life – often the same people – began to count the missing. Ten years previously, sexual freedom and drug use had been widely accepted, but now the troops were disappearing from the scene. Young men who had been pillars of the Palace vanished without a word. Former stars of night-life died at home, alone with their mothers. No-one closed the backrooms, and their proprietors refused to install condom dispensers, because they didn't want to scare the customers who came to dance and have sex – but the general carefree atmosphere had long-since vanished. Those who still met in small groups drew up a discreet, alarming tally of the lost. After such carnage, old address books were destined for the dustbin.

Gia Carangi, a beauty who had graced the cover of *Vogue*, died at the age of twenty-six in 1986, infected by an injection of heroin between two catwalk shows. Antonio Lopez, the gifted illustrator, and Karl Lagerfeld's companion for so many parties in Paris and joyful holidays in Saint-Tropez, died the following year at the age of forty-four. Juan Ramos, who used to take Karl round the bookshops of Saint-Germain-des-Prés to scour them for novels and art books, was HIV positive. So was Dennis Thim, the Paris correspondent of the fashion bible *Women's Wear Daily*. So was Xavier de Castella, Kenzo's partner with whom Jacques had organised the Moratoire noir(e). "A terrible list," wrote Karl Lagerfeld; "it gave the impression that everyone we knew was afflicted."

In New York, Corey Tippin was included in the same hecatomb. In the nightclubs, the atmosphere became gloomy as collections were organised in the middle of festivities for those suffering from AIDS. Andy Warhol died in 1987, following an operation, but almost all the deaths thereafter amongst former guests at the Factory were related to AIDS. Anyone who wished to survive had said goodbye to a carefree existence.

Lagerfeld was far too well-informed by his daily reading of the French, German and American papers not to be aware of how slowly research progressed. Suddenly, he understood his partner's inescapable fate. He telephoned the best doctors in Paris and the United States, all in vain. No treatment was available. In addition, the syndrome was then so little understood, in spite of the death toll, that each time Jacques had to go to hospital for tests, Karl noticed that the doctors "received him booted and wrapped up in protective clothing and masks, like doctors during the Great Plague in the Middle Ages." Lagerfeld – a man who hated sickness and death, who kept well away from any colleague with a mild cold – now took on Jako's care completely.

He was not entirely alone. "One day, I received a phone call from Armelle de Bascher. She wanted to tell me that her son was in Hôpital Bichat and was asking for me," Diane de Beauvau-Craon remembers. "I had no other horizon at the time than my addictions and my son, but I wanted to have time to think before I went to see Jacques. The next day but one I went to Bichat, and a new story began to unfold."

Karl and Diane embarked together on a very strange journey. When Jacques was in hospital, the couturier sent his Rolls round to collect Diane, so that she could take her daily turn at the bedside of their mutual friend, who seemed to be gradually dissolving. The hospital staff kept their distance, grouping the AIDS patients together as if they were in quarantine. "Do you want to catch it?" a nurse barked at Diane, when she saw her massaging Jacques's legs to prevent him getting ulcers. To get anywhere near the bed, a whole list of disclaimers had to be signed if you did not want to wear a terrifying cosmonaut costume that transported visitors to another planet.

Thanks to Karl's money and Diane's friendship with Dr Jacques Leibowitch, an immunology specialist working at the forefront of AIDS research, Jako was able to leave Bichat in 1988, and enter the infectious diseases department of Hôpital Raymond Poincaré in Garches, where the terror of the nursing staff was less visible. Lagerfeld visited nearly every evening, where he would meet Armelle de Bascher by Jacques's bedside. He had always got on well with her. She was authoritarian as a mother, possibly castrating – just as his own had been. He showered her with presents, handbags and Chanel jackets, armfuls of flowers. She had never complained that her son was viewed as Karl's gigolo. What a curious group around the hospital bed! It was the same, in fact, in each room: a cluster of former merrymakers, once-beautiful people and tearful mothers.

During remissions, Jacques rested at the family *château*, La Berrière. Karl Lagerfeld bought a new house for his convalescence, an hour from Paris at Mée-sur-Seine, in the Forêt de Fontainebleau. It was an enormous manor house measuring one thousand square metres, standing in a majestic wooded park. As usual, the couturier carried out some important alterations before proceeding with the elegant décor. If matters were urgent, a helicopter could land in and take off from the park. Friends who came to visit Jacques and Karl could also rest there between hospital visits.

The couturier continued with his frenetic professional life. He never abandoned his collections; he sketched at home every morning, went to fittings and never missed a dinner with the press. Only his chauffeur Brahim, who drove him to Garches in the late afternoon, knew of his double life. Karl talked all day about dresses and fashion, then spread optimism at the hospital in the evening. In happier times, Jacques had regaled him with snippets of gossip from the world and exciting tales of nightlife. Their roles were now reversed, and it was Karl who reported on the outside world to his friend, immobilised by transfusions. An exhausting way of life, certainly, but it was Karl's tribute to his impossible partner, for whom his love grew ever deeper.

It also meant that Lagerfeld discovered a new world. He had never wanted anything but to be surrounded by luxury, youth and beauty. No household chores, no destitution or squalor. Even his memories of the war – the wounded, the poor, the displaced – were tucked away in the far corners of his memory, never intruding into his private reality. In the hospital, things were different. Karl was astonished to see illness, weakness and poverty first-hand. After Jacques's first admission he paid for televisions to be installed in every room. He increased his gifts to the research workers and gave presents to the nurses. Money has no power over death, but he could at least help those who were still alive and struggling against its onslaught.

At the beginning of 1989, Jacques developed Karposi's sarcoma, a skin cancer frequent in those suffering from AIDS. In the depleted circles of gay men, these disfiguring purple spots were an alarming signal, and Jacques knew that he looked frightening: "He no longer looked at himself in the mirror, and made his face up with a mask of terracotta to allay suspicion," Diane observed; she was devastated. At La Berrière, Jacques kept a loaded gun in the bathroom to cover any eventuality. He continued to drink whisky by the litre, all the same – but he hardly ate. At the end of the spring, Karl had to go on a world tour to present the Chanel and Fendi collections. "If you gain three kilos, I'll give you an Aston Martin," he promised before he left, terrified by Jacques's weight loss. How did Karl give dozens of entertaining interviews, while constantly fielding calls that informed him of his partner's worsening condition?

Summer was a nightmare. In New York, two of Diane's other friends died from AIDS: the photographer Robert Mapplethorpe and Steve Rubell, the proprietor of Studio 54. In the apartment in Rue de Rivoli, Jacques was hooked up to an oxygen canister, but Diane had to call an ambulance, because he was suffocating in her arms. In bed again, he could hardly bear the pain of the oxygen mask against the raw skin of his nose. The treatments made him irascible; he could behave abominably to Karl and Diane, his mother, his brothers and sister, deafening them with morbid messages and suicidal ideation, then plunging into terrible bouts of despair.

Karl and Diane knew death was nearing – "but we both knew that we would be there for him until the end," Diane said. Jacques knew it too. He was saturated with medication, yet did not want to die. Then, one moment later, he would prepare his loved ones for his imminent disappearance. "During the final days, I slept on a camp bed in his room," Karl Lagerfeld told me. "Well, you could not really call it sleeping. It was abominable. My mother was right; you should not inflict the spectacle of your death on the living."

Jacques de Bascher, the dandy who embodied the free spirit of the '70s, died on 3 September 1989, at the age of thirty-eight. It was an exceedingly hot Sunday. Seated around his bed, Lagerfeld, Diane and Armelle de Bascher were with him to his final moment.

The cremation took place at Père-Lachaise, at a ceremony organised by the De Bascher family – but Karl Lagerfeld organised a second ceremony at Le Mée-sur-Seine the following day, in the chapel adjoining the handsome house he had bought for Jacques to convalesce in.

Jacques must have a mass – so decreed Lagerfeld, the great blasphemer, who liked the pomp and circumstance of church but didn't believe in God. The couturier had surrounded the altar with dozens of baskets of white lilies, as the deceased had declared himself a monarchist. Armelle de Bascher and her children sat in the front row (except for Anne, Jacques's sister, who was too shocked to attend the second ceremony, which seemed like a repeat of the first). On the other side of the aisle, at the same level, were Karl and Diane de Beauvau-Craon; there could have been no better way of indicating that Jacques had two families.

A few of Lagerfeld's colleagues had been informed by Brahim, the couturier's chauffeur. Princess Caroline came from Monaco, but none of Jacques's good-time friends had been invited. Yves Saint Laurent did not even send a message.

Jacques de Bascher had asked for his teddy bear, Michka, to be put in his coffin. The ashes were shared out: half for Armelle de Bascher, the other half for Karl. Karl had his half placed in an urn, bought in a sale room, which he then sealed and installed on top of a column in his huge apartment in the Rue des Saints-Pères. He requested that after his death, his own ashes were to be mingled with those of his mother and Jacques, and all of them thrown to the winds.

14

No-one had ever seen Karl Lagerfeld so unhappy. He was not usually a man to show his emotions. He never hugged you, or risked any kind of caress. His method of embracing you was to give you a thump on the shoulder. Since Jacques's death, however, he had ossified in his despair like a tree in ice. At the Chanel studio, his collaborators suspected when they saw his form shaking slightly that he was sobbing over his drawings. "I saw profound sorrow on Karl's face and a helplessness that I had never seen before," said his friend Florentine Pabst anxiously; she often came from Hamburg to comfort him.

Lagerfeld did not stop working, however. A few days after the funeral at Le Mée, he began drawing new collections for Chanel, Fendi and his own label, KL. But he became colder. With Jacques, he had vicariously enjoyed the kind of life he forbade himself from living, and the trade-off was mutual. Now, only his daily labours kept him upright.

Perhaps foreshadowing the change of rhythm provoked by Jacques's death, Karl had had a row some months previously with his muse, Inès de la Fressange. He refused to officially acknowledge that she had agreed to let her face be used as the mould for the bust of 'Marianne', the symbol of the French Republic, which was to be displayed in all French town halls. The fact that a Parisian woman with a noble name had been chosen as this emblem should have amused him, but he went on to declare in the *Herald Tribune* that "Marianne is the symbol of all that is boring, bourgeois and provincial." It was the first time he had publicly attacked Inès – who had contributed as much as he had to Chanel's image. The teams in Rue Cambon were petrified.

They had worked together for seven years, and, without being intimates, Inès and Karl certainly passed for friends. How many fittings had they sat through together? How many dinners in Rue de l'Université, tours for Chanel, weekends at the house in Le Mée, where they might be joined by Princess Caroline of Monaco, her husband Stefano Casiraghi and their children? "If one day I chuck out Inès, I shall chuck myself out with her," Karl had claimed on the television station France 2, a year after their collaboration began.

Karl's friendship was an intoxicating wine; you had to be careful with it. Presents, delicate attentions, witty remarks – he was a matchless companion. But, like him, you could never show weakness. "No-one could permit themselves to be sad, unwell or just tired; you could never relax, and I learned after a certain time that genuine conversation was impossible," Inès de la Fressange informs me today. At first, she went along with his reminisces of "My mother used to say that…", but she came to wonder more and more why he took such pleasure in pouring forth these invented stories. How could he go on repeating his stock of anecdotes, which she had come to know by heart? "He told me how, one day when he had told his mother that a man had tried to kiss him, he heard the following reply: 'Look at the way you are dressed and how you style your hair. You lit his fire!' But of course, he brushed aside any allusion to Sigmund Freud."

She let slip in the American press one day that he hated his hands, following his mother's tough criticism of them when he was a boy. She said she found it touching, the way he used to hide them under long sleeves. This might seem harmless, but Karl never allowed anyone but himself to talk about his childhood or his complexes. The anecdote was meant to be light and affectionate, but he took it for mockery – like the mockery he had heard behind his back fifteen years earlier from Corey, Pat and Donna, when he was walking down the street in mules, laden with trinkets. "I see, you're acting the little psychoanalyst," he shouted at her when she returned to the studio, the day after the article appeared. No introspection was permitted from his circle, and certainly no intimate revelations. After all, the most popular precept in fashion circles is *lightness*.

If Inès allowed herself little slips when she was with Lagerfeld, who never made any, it was because her mind was elsewhere. The muse was no longer entirely absorbed by Lagerfeld and the Chanel studio. At the age of thirty-two, she had met a lover, Luigi d'Urso. As a result, she was less inclined to put up with the couturier's prevarications when he insisted that the models and the workshop should wait for him for fittings that might last far into the night.

Luigi d'Urso was not impressed by Lagerfeld. Born into an upper-class family, he was both a businessman and an art dealer. Like many well-born Italians, he was always slightly scornful of Germans. He was as cultivated as Karl, but unlike him, he liked going out, drinking and dancing. When the couple were invited to La Vigie, Luigi raised an eyebrow at the fitted carpet in the splendid Italianate villa's rooms. He commented, "That's unusual in a house in the South." Karl, showing him his office, began boasting about his cylindrical desk – "a splendid piece of richly ornamented furniture, of which there is only one other example…" – and Luigi finished the sentence, with a superior look: "… in the king's little apartment in the Château de Versailles." The two men definitely did not get on.

Rivalry, irritation, jealousy – or a mixture of all three. In France as abroad, the image of Inès de la Fressange was much more widely recognised that that of Karl Lagerfeld. She was the one associated with Chanel, not him. Every day, an impressive number of letters addressed to her arrived in Rue Cambon, and were placed in the studio, just behind Karl's table. "In the street, when we were walking along together, I was the one who was stopped to be told 'I adore what you're doing'," she finishes. "He had put on weight, in his business suits. He was no longer an icon."

The business with the Marianne bust was only a pretext, but it was not taken lightly in Rue Cambon. As soon as the misunderstanding had filtered into the microcosm of the fashion world, an extraordinary meeting was organised between Karl and Inès with Chanel's director of communication, Marie-Louise de Clermont-Tonnerre and the head of fashion, Françoise Montenay. The two women wanted to convince the model not to pose for the emblem of the Republic, "because Karl doesn't want you to." But things soured quickly. Karl provokingly suggested that, at the next catwalk show, this false Marianne should wear a dress patterned with fleur de lis. "I will not," retorted Inès, in front of everybody.

Lagerfeld always wanted to have the last word. Although in 1984, Inès had signed an exceptional contract for 300,000 dollars a year, regularly increased since then, he forbade the star Chanel model from taking part in the July collection show. Worse, he began publishing disobliging remarks about her in the press. Inès de la Fressange had committed an unforgivable blunder: she had treated Karl as the 'Kaiser', a nickname he only half liked, as he was aware of the anti-German feeling in France. "I do not intend to work with her again," he said in *Le Figaro*. "It's simple: she no longer inspires me." Before adding: "Without me, she would still be running from photo session to photo session like all the others, with her book." Was she not the image of Chanel? "Yes, that was true for the 1980s. But in fact, her reputation is very local. She has never been on the cover of *Vogue* in the

States. Her Parisian microcosm, her champagne socialist side, is very limited," Karl jibed, before adding what he thought would be the finishing blow: "I don't dress listed buildings."

After that, every time he was asked about his former muse, he would tell a humiliating anecdote: "She was always late." In *Paris Match,* he claimed that "She despised the people in the studio," before suggesting: "As the German proverb says, Inès goes after money like the devil after the soul. In March last year, after the show, she flung herself on Alain Wertheimer in front of everybody, and asked for a pay rise." Not true, of course. But Karl always went for a violent, brutal break. The former muse even suspects him of "slipping the fact to *Le Point* and *L'Express* that I was a tax exile in Great Britain…"

Losing Inès de la Fressange under such circumstances was bad news for Chanel, but no-one dared contradict Lagerfeld. Alain Wertheimer didn't say a word to the poor victim. Everyone in the studio kept quiet. A few months earlier, Chanel had sent their star model to dine with the European sales directors, or to appear in front of saleswomen in Seattle or Atlanta. Now, it was as if she had suddenly disappeared. "The rights were all on his side," she told me. "I had been disowned and they all followed."

She was not the first to pay a high price for Karl's temper. He always got rid of his successive circles, just as he made a clean sweep whenever he moved house. Antonio Lopez, Anna Piaggi, Inès de la Fressange… "I bleach out my past," he used to say. After the death of Jacques, he became harder, his cruel irony more biting.

He mixed little with other dress designers. At the beginning of the '90s, Robert Altman planned to set his next film, *Prêt-à-porter*, in the Paris fashion world. He hired Nathalie Rykiel as his artistic consultant. Rykiel had already organised lunches for the American film maker with Christian Lacroix, Gianfranco Ferré, Claude Montana, Thierry Mugler and Jean-Paul Gaultier, who all made guest appearances in the film. Only Karl Lagerfeld refused to take part in this programme; he instead invited Altman, Sonia and Nathalie Rykiel to a sumptuous dinner at his house. "Bob Altman was wonderful, and with Karl, this wasn't easy," Nathalie Rykiel told me. "As we went out, when he thought he had won, I had to tell him: 'Did you understand that he will not take part in the film?' At dinner, Bob ran through the list of couturiers who had agreed to appear in *Prêt-à-porter* and I immediately saw Lagerfeld's face. He was not at the centre of the film and it was quite clear that he would not do it…"

Until then, he had been admired for his work ethic, his inventiveness and his scathing humour. So long as he ruled over Chanel, he was feared. One day he was told that a press attaché assigned to the house had rather clumsily assured a journalist that "The collection is more beautiful this year than last." He dismissed him on the spot. Another who sat in an empty place in the front row of the catwalk show was thanked in the same way the next day, as was an intern who allowed a photograph to be published without Karl's validation.

With the power inherent in being the Kaiser of fashion, Karl could break a career and vindictively pursue those who failed him: "I know it is despicable and horrible, but I do not see why I should not pay people back in their own currency, if they have done something bad to me," he wrote in his small book of aphorisms – then emphasised in larger letters: "I pull back the chair when they have forgotten everything – maybe ten years later."

This is how the emperor of fashion surrounded himself with a court of faithful followers – and a line of exiles, a few metres away. These were the people who had formerly inspired him, collaborators who ended by taking up too much space, courtiers from the past who did not grasp the boundaries between fidelity and slavery. Now that Karl had lost the man he loved, his professional life had to stand in for family life. Watch out anyone trying to escape his grasp.

When you meet these former favourites who were sent packing, their ambivalence about Lagerfeld is striking. They are always split between regret for his enchanted way of life, and bitterness at having been excluded from it so brutally. Lagerfeld had two faces. He could be the most attentive of friends – when Stefano Casiraghi, the husband of Princess Caroline, was killed in a racing yacht off the coast at Saint-Jean-Cap-Ferrat, he telephoned his friend nearly every day, sending tender letters illustrated with little entertaining drawings, a present, flowers; lending her Le Mée to escape to.

The other side of his character was shadier, possessive and harsh. As someone who had always insisted that others should be as disciplined as he was, was he still capable of a selfless gesture? The dismissal of Inès de la Fressange, who everyone thought unassailable, was a warning. How could anyone part from him on good terms, when he would not put up with the slightest infidelity?

Gilles Dufour, director of the Chanel studio, was approached one day by another fashion house. Lagerfeld learnt about it, and without saying anything, he put a note on Dufour's desk on which he had written the other house's name. "You don't leave Karl," Victoire de Castellane remarked. After fourteen years in the 'magic studio', Gilles Dufour's niece also wanted to leave. She was married with three children and hoped for a private life, far away from those interminable fitting sessions when the couturier would not arrive before 8pm, forcing all the studio to work another full day, which would never end until the middle of the night. Up to that point, he could find no words affectionate enough to describe the young woman's originality and talent. But as she was bound for Dior, he immediately wrote 'Dior is Chanel's dustbin!' in the papers. Gilles Dufour left six months later. A flood of criticism immediately followed, a systematic denigration in the fashion world where reputations are so quickly destroyed. His niece was right. You don't leave Karl.

Even the loyal Caroline Lebar had to confront the wrath of the gods. One day, she admitted to Karl that Christian Lacroix had offered to employ her at three times the salary. "OK, you can leave at once!" he said, wounded. "I had to wait for a week, until he came back from New York to tell him that I wasn't leaving," she told me. He appointed her as press attaché immediately and gave her a substantial pay rise.

Karl Lagerfeld liked a bit of opposition, but only to a certain degree. At the heart of KL, the studio director Céline Engle finally married Ralph Toledano, the director general. "Meeting your husband at work, Karl's ideal scenario," laughed Engle, a former dancer who had become a stylist. It was her job to sort through the hundreds of drawings Karl provided, which helped to build their collection; he grew more and more irritated when she rejected some of his choices. "I've designed for the wastepaper basket, bring me the wastepaper basket!" he would order. He refused to listen, grumbling at every decision she made.

How could he tell this young woman about her fall from grace? Across his different fashion houses, Karl Lagerfeld had always amused himself by drawing his colleagues, giving them cartoons of themselves as if they were presents. One day, he arrived with his arms full of cakes and champagne, in excellent humour. During the fittings, he sat down and – as usual – began sketching each collaborator, this time as a character from the Ancien Régime. Aristocrats in silk stockings, princesses in dresses with panniers; everyone could recognise their own features in this heap of paper.

It was Céline's turn to be sketched. First, Karl drew a face. Then a hand above the face holding a clump of hair. When he held out the drawing for her to see, she discovered her severed head with the words: 'To Céline, in memory of this collection'. The following day, via her husband, she received a gigantic basket of flowers to confirm the termination of her contract.

Nevertheless, who could refuse to work in Lagerfeld's wake? Everything he touched saw success. The money seemed limitless. When he took all his collaborators from Paris to Monaco, the whole team stayed at the Monte-Carlo Beach, one of the best hotels in the city-state. He himself led a luxurious life. Rolls-Royce, private jet. Could he remember how many houses and apartments he owned? He endlessly bought and sold – it was another way of pulling the wool over his observers' eyes.

After Jacques de Bascher's death, Karl gave up Grand-Champ, the Breton castle that had been their joint project. He hardly ever went there. He agreed to open the property for the British Queen Mother during a trip she was making to France, to take tea and visit the park, filling the house with flowers for the occasion. Imagine showing such a castle, with its luxurious arrangements, to someone who had lived through the Blitz!

When the Queen Mother returned to her side of the Channel, Grand-Champ was closed up again, inhabited only by Pilar and Rafael, the faithful couple who had looked after Elisabeth Lagerfeld. In the absence of Jacques, the property lacked the attraction it once held. Karl had a fleeting plan to start work on it again, but abandoned the enterprise. "A house means nothing to me because I have no family," he told his friends. He sent the removal vans in one day without going back.

To Patrick Hourcade, who had supervised the restoration of the property, the digging of the ponds, the decoration of Elisabeth Lagerfeld's bedroom and the construction of the staircase that led to Jacques's bedroom in the attic, Karl simply observed: "You see, I'm tearing out the pages of a book." When this friend repudiated, writing him a letter full of sadness at his choice, Karl replied, implacably: "At any rate, I shall never be happy."

Jacques de Bascher liked Germany and Hamburg far more than Lagerfeld did. He had often suggested to Karl that, as a final reconciliation with his past, he should buy his parents' house. Now Jacques was dead, Karl Lagerfeld decided to invest in a magnificent villa on the banks of the Elbe, in Blankenese, on the outskirts of Hamburg, where Otto and Elisabeth had lived.

The house was a vast grey building adorned with classical columns, surrounded by 12,000 square metres of parkland. From the terrace, you had the impression that you could dive straight into the river. Karl himself designed the large high-backed green velvet sofas that graced the salon of 'Villa Jako', as he immediately named it. He never really wanted to stay there. "On his first visit," Patrick Hourcade told me, "an elderly gentleman rang on the doorbell. 'Wie geht's?' [How are you?] It was a friend from school. Karl was appalled."

"It is a mistake to try and reconnect with your past" – regretting his purchase, Karl was soon determined to sell the villa. The only posthumous gift to Jacques is a photograph by Jean-Marie Périer, who had suggested making a trip to Hamburg with Karl. Snow covered the front steps and the park. So, in a flash of inspiration, the photographer asked the driver of the car to come and sit beside his subject, with his back turned. Karl sits there, erect and sombre under a black umbrella. Behind his shoulder is what looks like Jacques's shadow...

15

It was the end of an era for fashion. The carefree life was over, leaving only a scatter of sequins on the catwalks. Not only were people growing less optimistic, but the fashion trade was at a crossroads. Money had wormed its way in everywhere. Sales were now the motivating factor. Ten years earlier, evening parties were held for the pleasure of dancing, laughing, taking drugs and sleeping with the other guests. Now, parties were thrown to launch perfumes.

Was it his fear of being swept away by the winds of change that made Karl Lagerfeld renew his style and inspiration? After Inès de la Fressange, he threw in his lot with her direct opposite: a beautiful, sexy blonde, German like him. At just twenty, Claudia Schiffer looked like the dream au pair girl; she was mobbed every time she appeared. "I made her," Karl was to say later. It was not entirely true. Two years earlier, her striking resemblance to Brigitte Bardot and an advertising campaign for jeans that were available worldwide had burned her silhouette into everyone's retinae. She already had an agent and a chauffeur, and two or three of her family members worked as her dressers and assistants.

Karl Lagerfeld had hitherto had the long, thin Inès in mind when he designed his collections for Chanel. How could he dress Claudia's curves? "Her bust was too big for dresses, her hips too large for straight skirts," was Gilles Dufour's comment. "Basically, she looked fantastic in the nude." Claudia provided a new source of inspiration for Lagerfeld. Forget long straight dresses and braided jackets; he had her modelling pale pink tweed mini shorts with a little open jacket, the Chanel monogram hanging on a chain between her breasts.

Claudia was too forthright to reply to the journalists as la Fressange did – but she was breathtakingly beautiful, co-operative and very professional. With this bourgeois young lady from the Rhineland, Karl showed the world that he could still handle a breath of modernity.

This was essential now that fashion had been transformed into a huge market place. "In the mid-nineties, the big financial corporations took over the independent fashion houses; fashion became industrialised and words ending in 'y' like creativity, femininity were replaced by words ending in 'ing' like marketing," Jean-Jacques Picart noted; he was a legendary press attaché who became consultant to a number of fashion moguls. More than ever, the couturiers had to be accountable to their shareholders.

Karl responded to this better than anyone else. One of his qualities was a remarkable instinct for self-preservation. Jacques de Bascher had a taste for flamboyant destruction, Karl for survival in a storm. Eight times a year the proprietor of Chanel, Alain Wertheimer held a meeting either in New York, where he lived, or in Paris, of the five regional heads of his group and the leaders of his fashion, perfumery and beauty businesses.

You only need to look at the turnover and profits to make sense of this. Haute couture had gone under and bore no resemblance to the scene Lagerfeld had known at the outset, in 1954. Too elitist and, above all, such a loss-maker. However, it was a better showcase than prêt-à-porter for selling accessories, shoes, lipstick and perfume. With a handbag there was never any problem of the customer's size, and the returns were excellent.

"When I go into a shop, I look for the clothes… Today, they are on the first floor and the accessories on the ground floor," Hubert de Givenchy lamented in private; he decided to retire in 1995. Karl Lagerfeld never wasted tears over worlds that no longer existed, and was perfectly able to make his collections into a communicative tool: "Fashion is to look forward," he used to say to the editor of *Vogue*, Anna Wintour. He made this into a philosophy: 'Change is the healthiest way to survive'.

At the end of summer 1992, Lagerfeld was approached to re-join Chloé, the label he had left ten years earlier to take over Chanel. Losing momentum, the prêt-à-porter label wanted to revive the splendour of the 1970s, the time when the couturier had produced the light and airy dresses that contributed so fruitfully to building its name. After weeks of secret negotiations, he was appointed artistic director of Chloé. The Vendôme Group, now owners of Chloé, offered him a fabulously lucrative four-year contract and bought Karl Lagerfeld SA for tens of millions of euros.

Chanel, Fendi, KL, Chloé: from now on he was designing and managing the communications of four fashion houses, surrounded by an army of financiers and lawyers. He never seemed satisfied. "Nothing gives me any pleasure, I'm frigid. I'm like a nymphomaniac for work," he told the newspapers. In the morning he would rise at 5am in his huge apartment on the Rue de l'Université. The butler would prepare his breakfast and he would draw for his 'labels' until 9am.

This was also a means of carrying on. The world around him was experiencing a radical face-lift. In 1993, Pierre Bergé, whose aim was to build his own group with Yves Saint Laurent, sold to Sanofi. The Bergé-Saint Laurent partnership held on to control of the couture house, but relinquished – for a lot of money – the lucrative perfume and cosmetics sectors. Yves had never fully recovered from his tumultuous affair with De Bascher, and since then had ricocheted from stunningly beautiful collections to bouts of severe depression. He was beginning to talk like Gabrielle Chanel, when she denounced the mini skirt: "This morning, I met a very pretty girl wearing a skirt that was only 40cm wide. Her suspenders were showing under her skirt. Be naked, be dressed, but don't be like that!" Saint Laurent lamented in 1993.

Karl would never have spoken like this – he was eager to understand every new twist and turn, to absorb changes that came about during his lifetime, to surf every wave. Two years earlier, he was the first to install travelling rails along the catwalk at Chanel so that the cameras could film the models in motion. Girls dressed by Karl wore jeans, carried quilted denim bags, wore net tee-shirts that revealed their breasts and – on top of it all – sported a golden cap worn backwards, like rappers or street walkers.

Lagerfeld had experienced the modernisation of an artisanal profession in the '60s and '70s, had taken part in its financial mutation and industrialisation, and was not about to be pushed out. A few new faces had arrived in his world. Bernard Arnault, a tall, cool ex-student of the École Polytechnique, had made his entry into fashion by buying up almost everything that was anything over the past fifteen years. Karl Lagerfeld would sometimes recite the list from memory: in 1993, the famous year when Saint Laurent had complained of the ugliness of the street, Bernard Arnault, already head of Dior and Louis Vuitton within the LVMH group, bought Berluti and Kenzo. The only property retained by the Japanese designer, who used to dance with Jacques at the Palace, was his full name: Kenzo Takada.

The following year, Arnault bought Guerlain perfumes. In 1996 and 1997, he absorbed Loewe, Marc Jacobs and Sephora, one after another. Then in 1999, the British shirtmaker Thomas Pink fell into his lap, along with the cosmetics company Make Up For Ever and the Italian Emilio Pucci, the 'Prince of Prints'. The following year he absorbed Fendi and the fashion house of the American stylist Donna Karan, DKNY, and in 2001, La Samaritaine.

Karl Lagerfeld was also able to list the acquisitions of the industrialist François Pinault, who abandoned the wood trade to launch himself into the luxury industries. Thirteen years older than Arnault, an art-lover from Brittany, Pinault and his group PPR (Pinault-Printemps-Redoute) acquired, from 1995, the brands Gucci, Yves Saint Laurent, Boucheron, Bottega Veneta and Alexander McQueen. The economic press now employs journalists specialising in the 'luxury industries' to keep an eye on this mind-blowing whirlwind.

In addition to the industrial transformation, this also represented an intellectual and affective change, a transformation of habits. "Previously, you would invite Saint Laurent, Lagerfeld and Givenchy to dinner and the evening would be a success. Then it was Claudia Schiffer, Inès de la Fressange and Cindy Crawford. Now you have to invite Arnault and Pinault," the socialite Ira de Fürstenberg complained to her friends.

Lagerfeld reached the age of sixty in 1993 but, in the eyes of the new fashion tycoons, he was a sort of model entrepreneur who could foretell the future, an all-rounder. He drew, created and communicated – and, since 1987, took photographs of his own designs for press-books and advertisements, adapting himself to the styles of the different fashion houses he worked for. 'Art director' was the profession he embodied, the prototype of a modern creator who contributed on every level and could invent the whole identity of a brand. "He did a great disservice to fashion by making us believe that a designer could work for two or three brands at the same time," his colleagues would lament.

His days were endless. The designer would rise at 5am to design his collections, but designing now only occupied half his time. The other half was spent in communication and publicity – world tours in a private aeroplane, photo sessions and interviews: no other stylist expended so much energy. "I can see him so clearly, during a promotional tour in Asia for KL," Ralph Toledano, then director of the company, remembers. "In Japan, Hong Kong he was welcomed like a king, Rolls at the airport and huge hotel suite. But when he arrived in Singapore he was overwhelmed by the stifling, humid heat. And the people putting plastic necklaces round his neck... He wanted to get back into his aeroplane straight away. We finally met at the Hilton... Brahim, his chauffeur, had managed to convince him to have a siesta. Then the guy from the local daily paper comes in earlier than expected!" Toledano was even more amazed when he witnessed Brahim telling Lagerfeld from behind his bedroom door that "The Mayor of Singapore has arrived!" to make him get out of bed. "Half an hour later, Karl came in looking impeccable. The journalist facing him was used to dealing with dogs being squashed in road accidents and knew nothing about fashion. But Karl gave him an hour-long interview, ultra-professional, and the guy was delighted."

Karl always had to be aware of the danger of being side-lined. In 1995, Bernard Arnault introduced the British designer John Galliano to Givenchy. By the following year, Galliano was with Dior. What a sudden threat to Karl! Each collection by the new *enfant terrible* of fashion was hailed as a great event. Each dress was crazily inventive. The fabrics were airy and the cut sexy and poetic. Galliano also had an acute feeling for publicity. His catwalk shows were built like an inexorable planetary war machine. All the papers were talking about his incredibly thin models being transformed into sublime squaws or Masai warriors, eighteenth-century maids or female bullfighters. Photographs of Princess Diana, who opened an exhibition celebrating fifty years of the house of Dior at the Metropolitan Museum of Art, New York, wearing one of the first dresses designed by Galliano, went global. Since his arrival, sales at Dior had quadrupled.

In 1998, Karl Lagerfeld approached Galliano's muse, Amanda Harlech. She was an elegant British woman, married to an aristocrat who had a seat in the House of Lords. Two of her sisters-in-law, Alice and Jane, had inspired Eric Clapton and the Rolling Stones. "You will be my third eye," Karl told her, offering her a staggering contract. Then, as he did not want to have an argument with 'John', he suggested a better solution: she would work for them both. This gave him the illusion that his 'third eye' was primarily a telescope that allowed him to see what his rival was preparing.

The new master of the fashion world, Bernard Arnault, was not only an aggressive manager, but also a good judge of character. Seeing Karl fight like that in order not to let Galliano get ahead awakened his interest and a kind of admiration. So, it was to Karl he went first when, in 2000, he planned to buy Fendi. "I realised straight away that he was the key to future success," he said. In a salon stuffed with works of art, at the Dior headquarters in Avenue Montaigne, the boss of LVMH remembers the questions he asked at the time. The Fendi sisters were not getting on and were battling over whether or not to sell the family business. "Karl was the only person who could succeed in getting them together," he told me. "He pleaded the cause of LVMH and later it was his presence alone in the company that held it together. I know very few men who combine, as he does, creative genius with organisational ability."

Lagerfeld was no longer just a designer. He had also become a consultant-in-the-shadows to the great fashion magnates, particularly Arnault. With the Wertheimer brothers, conversations were always somewhat stilted, even though Karl adored their mother, Éliane Heilbronn. The Arnaults were a slightly more accessible family. At this level of power, mingling professional with social relations was a rule for survival. With his culture and his humour, Lagerfeld impressed the big boss. Arnault remains extremely rich; no-one can rival him in France.

But Lagerfeld offered special little details. The captain of LVMH has a passion for music? The couturier invited him to his house in Rue de l'Université, that eighteenth-century Parisian palace, all gold and silk velvet. In one salon he had two pianos installed, side by side, so that Arnault could come and play there with his wife Hélène, a concert pianist.

The marriage of Delphine Arnault, daughter of the king of luxury, to an Italian heir in 2005 took place at Château d'Yquem, near Bordeaux, the property of LVMH. A handful of members of the government – including Nicolas Sarkozy, then Minster of the Interior, and his economic counterpart Thierry Breton – thronged the church, followed by most of the tycoons of CAC 40, and the British singer Elton John. How could a guest stand out? At the entrance to the *château*, Lagerfeld installed a photographic studio where guests were invited to pass in front of his lens: that was his wedding present.

In another stroke of genius, he was one of the few people to maintain a cordial relationship with François Pinault, the eternal rival of the president of LVMH, at the same time. "It happened that I needed to ask his advice on one of his colleagues," the boss of Kering (ex-PPR) told me recently. The star-studded evening parties hosted by Karl Lagerfeld give some measure of his ambition. The little dinners of yesteryear, in the kitchen around a plate of sausages and another plate of cheese, no longer really existed. They gave way to sumptuous dinner parties in his grand rooms, organised with the help of Françoise

Dumas, the high priestess of events management. 'Under the sign of the fish' was the theme for one of his annual parties. Not that Karl believed in astrology, but the title gave him a pretext for inviting the Belgian billionaire Albert Frère and Betty Lagardère, both born under the same star sign. Of course, Betty brought her husband, Jean-Luc Lagardère – boss of, among other things, *Paris Match* and *Elle*.

Lagerfeld designed the invitation cards for the Bal de la Rose, which, every year in Monaco, was attended by a large contingent from the Almanac de Gotha. At birthdays, all these 'friends' would receive huge bunches of flowers accompanied by a little portrait sketched by the master and a handwritten note.

All of this was highly skilled. Some people in fashion were slow to grasp the degree to which the world had changed. Independent fashion houses were going under. In 1995, the lingerie designer Chantal Thomass was sacked by her main Japanese shareholder and lost the right to use her name commercially.

'My patron', is how Christian Lacroix referred to Bernard Arnault… with some naiveté. After several years of losing money, the patron of LVMH let him go in 2005. "He created dreamy dresses, but they were only for museums," he says today. "Karl Lagerfeld, on the other hand, produced a huge profit globally."

This made Lagerfeld a true workaholic. In New York, where the couturier was going for Fashion Week, he stayed in a suite at The Pierre, a palace looking out on Central

Park. The day after the Chanel show, he flew off to Rome, where he spent a week designing the Fendi collection. At the weekend he photographed his clothes in one of his houses, or in Rue de Lille in Paris, in the studio he had furnished in front of his gigantic bookshelves, filled with art books and literature.

His teams ran around after him all week in Paris. The KL team would telephone the Chloé team, who would then call Chanel: 'Where is he?' The couture workshops waited for him for hours. "I had a file full of songs and we used to sing as we waited," recalled Anita Briey, then head of the KL studio. "All the seamstresses were furious. Then he would arrive at about 10pm and they were all delighted."

He was respected for his expertise in the trade, and admired for his culture and intelligence. His generosity was legendary. Karl Lagerfeld had clung on to his way of binding people to him by giving them opulent presents. He slipped an envelope of banknotes to a young apprentice to pay his rent, offered one of his many houses to a colleague for his holidays, and brought plates of cheese, cakes and sweets to the workshop. He ate, too. That was his way of drowning stress: in litres of Pepsi cola and mountains of Frankfurters, which still tasted to him of his childhood.

What was the couturier looking for in this frenzy of contracts, travel and dinners with the captains of industry? "Consolation," Diane de Beauvau-Craon would like to think. "Power and money, without a doubt," is Ralph Toledano's opinion. Since the early 1990s, money had been flowing into fashion. The luxury trade had become the leader of the French economy and one of the focal points of global finance. In former times, the couturiers lived like the upper middle classes. Now the most prominent designers were multi-millionaires.

Everyone agrees on one point at least: in 1999, Alain Belot, Lagerfeld's lawyer, met Dominique Strauss-Kahn in a discreetly situated office at the Ministry of Industry in order to negotiate a tax adjustment for the couturier. And it was also there that Belot slipped the Minister for the Economy a cassette tape, on which Jean-Claude Méry described the secret financing of the RPR (the French Republican Party) and the President Jacques Chirac's electoral campaigns.

Karl Lagerfeld could have easily avoided the following imbroglio, which, in 2000, shone a bright light on his attempts at tax avoidance. Since he moved to Monaco, the French revenue had gone over his contracts and his opulent lifestyle with a fine-toothed comb. They had discovered a flaw: La Vigie, the splendid villa on the shores of the Mediterranean, assumed to be in Monégasque territory, was in fact situated... in Roquebrune-Cap-Martin, France.

After Jacques Chirac's election to the Élysée in 1995, Lagerfeld grew close to his wife Bernadette, a 'friend' whom he invited to dinner frequently and dressed. Soon thereafter, he was granted a record tax exemption... But his accountant, Lucien Frydlender, continued his sophisticated financial operations. If the scandal of the Méry cassette had not broken out, who would have known that Dominique Strauss-Kahn had granted him a further reduction of 160 million francs and raised his tax adjustment to 46 million?

This time, Karl had to pay. Lagerfeld had to sell his furniture and paintings; the sale at Christie's lasted three days. The remaining tax bill was paid off by none other than the Wertheimer family.

16

What did that fortune-teller in Rue de Maubeuge say, twenty-five years ago, when Karl went to see her with Yves and Pierre? "It will begin for you when it ends for the others."

Well, that moment had come. Saint Laurent was no longer designing; the end was nigh. One evening, Inès de la Fressange went to have dinner with him. He ordered fruit juice as an aperitif: "If I drink alcohol, I see spiders and snakes in the night."

Until now, 'the little prince of fashion' (as he had been known thirty years earlier) had dominated everything. His tuxedos and his safari suits had won their place in the fashion pantheon. Women revered him. He had won every honour and earned a great deal of money. But, as he told the *New York Times* very frankly in December 2000, "I no longer have any sexuality. And it is damaging to creativity. No alcohol, no sex, it is very, very difficult to be creative." His Pygmalion, Pierre Bergé made the point in a different way: "The new financiers want to make money immediately. (…) One thing is missing from their makeup: a soul."

François Pinault, the new proprietor of YSL couture, appointed Tom Ford to be its head. Ford was an American, born in Texas, keen on architecture and well-versed in advertising. While Yves dreamed of re-creating Proustian elegance, Ford was the king of porno chic, which he had introduced successfully at Gucci. During his catwalk shows, the critics and fashion editors were no longer the only ones who mattered. The financial analysts at JPMorgan also published their opinion. In their eyes, Ford's collections were 'smart', 'hyper modern' – even 'safe'. 'They should sell well'. Yves no longer understood his times.

On 7 January 2002, Yves Saint Laurent said goodbye to fashion: "I am also saying goodbye to those aesthetic ghosts." Karl watched him give his farewells on the television, his right hand gripping the table: "I have been through so much anguish, so many depths of hell. I have known fear and terrible solitude. Sedatives and drugs, those false friends. The dungeon of depression and the prison of clinics." Karl listened to that childish, halting voice, and saw the ravaged looks. At sixty-five, Yves looked like an old man who still dyed his hair.

This slackening, this nostalgia and self-pity, this constant depression – "such an error of taste!" – it was everything Lagerfeld detested. Yves visited his psychoanalyst several times a week. Karl maintained that such a practice "kills creativity. If you are honest with yourself, you know the questions and answers. I don't need a psychoanalyst because I know the answers."

So far, Karl had avoided criticising Saint Laurent, but

now he had attained power, his views were sought after. He commented on Saint Laurent's departure with a cruelty that exposed the forty years of rivalry between them. "Balenciaga retired with more discretion, and Chanel died still making clothes. Frankly, he's not old enough. But to tell the truth, I don't give a toss. He won't be missed, and they are lucky to have Tom Ford. Bravo Tom!" When Karl talked like that, in his accent that rapped out his words like a blacksmith's hammer, the ghost of his mother could be heard, berating his childish weaknesses.

What a relief, all the same, not to have Yves Saint Laurent perched one step above him! Perhaps that was the main key to Lagerfeld's exceptional longevity: he outranked Saint Laurent in sheer staying power. He did not overtake him in the pantheon of couturiers, where YSL was unassailable – but he outlived him. Suzy Menkes, the fashion journalist of the *International Herald Tribune*, made a comparison between the two designers' legendary competition and the rivalry between 'Mozart and Salieri'. Lagerfeld's response was that "Salieri had a better life." At last, he could allow himself not to be on a war footing: if Yves had been king, now Karl truly was the Kaiser.

We must take a careful look at the diet Karl followed in the year 2000, when Saint Laurent first started to withdraw. Ten kilos lost, then twenty, then thirty. Most of Karl's assistants in the KL studio and at Chanel had to follow the same draconian low-calorie programme, like courtiers forcing themselves to comply with their overlord's latest whim. No-one could match his discipline.

Lagerfeld had a goal that outflanked all other motivations. Hedi Slimane's first catwalk show for Dior began on 28 January 2001. This tall, sophisticated Frenchman, who had wanted to be a journalist at *Le Monde* before opting for fashion, was the Bergé-Saint Laurent duo's new protégé. Both were there, seated at the front, in the row reserved for the stars. Karl Lagerfeld lurked somewhere in the wings with his camera, witnessing the birth of this new fashion genius, as consecrated by his rival partnership. He made a promise to himself: "Still ten kilos to lose. Maybe more… I want to be the first to wear this collection." Six months later he could fit into Slimane's narrow suits. It was as if he had eaten up Saint Laurent.

Forty-two kilos lost in thirteen months. This was the first step in Karl's twenty-first-century transformation. After ten years spent feasting on sausages and cake, he had become an imposing pasha, disguising his corpulence under Yohji Yamamoto's ample shirts. He was about to turn seventy: he had to get younger! From now on, Kaiser Karl wore mittens to hide the age spots on his hands, jeans with fitted jackets, large pectoral crucifixes on chains and death's head rings, like a rocker. He also wore fine boots, hand-made by Massaro, which he ordered 'nice and tight' to remind himself constantly of the need for maintenance. "Small clothes are better than weighing scales," he cried. "Nothing is more horrible than trousers that won't fasten."

Wherever he found a looking glass, Karl now eyed himself with delight. "Narcissism is a good thing," he wrote. "It stops you letting yourself go, it's nothing more than an instinct for self-preservation." Rather than returning to body-building ("which would be ridiculous at my age") he started learning the tango with a private tutor who taught him in his enormous eighteenth-century drawing room. What was the point of all this effort? "I just want to be a good coat hanger," he said, a tinge of self-mockery concealing his fear of encroaching age. Even his closest friend, the South African Ingrid Sischy – the former editor-in-chief of *Interview*, Andy Warhol's magazine, who conducted the interview that prefaced the book in which he explained his diet – did not dare ask *that* particular question. Now slim and satisfied with his appearance, Karl was ready to face his final challenge: to become a global icon.

If we want to pinpoint the exact moment when 'Kaiser Karl' transformed himself into the character everyone recognised, from New York to Pekin, we need to pause in spring 2004. The second stage. On this particular day, in the huge white salon on the first floor of his mansion, he laid on a sumptuous lunch. Iranian caviar in big black salad bowls, fine wines, porcelain plates and crystal glasses, flowers everywhere… He himself hardly ate anything, but the couturier wanted to impress his Swedish guests. Margareta van den Bosch, art director of H&M, had come from Stockholm, accompanied by her managing director and her marketing director. It was quite bold to present this interior, worthy of a court under the Ancien Régime, to the kings of bargain basement fashion.

Imposing, always dressed in black, the patron of 'chic and cheap' fashion was seldom intimidated. She reigned with a rod of iron over the hundred or so designers whose mission it was to renew the collections of the 1,700 H&M stores every season. It was her idea to invite Lagerfeld to surprise customers and boost sales. She hoped to seduce him.

Six months earlier, wearing her usual librarian-like glasses, Margareta van den Bosch had read the results of the international survey she had commissioned. "Karl Lagerfeld is the best-known name in the world," she informed her teams. "All the others are too old, or dead." Now that she had convinced the Perssons – father and son, the proprietors and bosses of the company – she wanted to ensure that their partnership would be a success.

Margareta knew men well, beyond the scope of any marketing survey. Karl Lagerfeld was seventy-one years old; he had received all the accolades and had a lot of money. As usual, he dazzled with his humour and detailed knowledge of Scandinavian literature. But his youthful elegance, the leather mittens hiding his hands and the white collar hiding his neck gave the impression from the outset that the war he waged was impossible to win. "Everyone comes into our stores," said Margareta. Then, cannily: "Young people, lots of young people." Lagerfeld found the offer irresistible. Before long, he signed the lucrative contract, making him the first haute couture designer to take on a collection of clothing that retailed at under 150 euros.

When the H&M stores opened their doors on 12 November 2004, long queues waited on the pavement outside. In Rue de Rivoli, Paris, Lagerfeld's clothes were presented in the basement – the crowd of excited people made it almost impossible to breathe. Hysteria was everywhere, captured by the television news.

The Swedish company had conjured up some witty, provocative publicity in English to advertise this collection, designed by one of the great names in couture, worldwide. In a panelled interior decorated with chandeliers – recollecting, perhaps, the lunch held in the white salon at Rue de l'Université – two absurd ageing snobs are seen choking on their caviar-filled eggs. "But it is impossible? Karl, is it true?" "Of course it's true," responds an imperturbable Lagerfeld, who requested to play himself. Faced with an ossified elite, he aimed to mark his entry into a different era: mass consumption, fast and ephemeral. H&M announced a 24 per cent boost in sales that month. Lagerfeld's sequins and little black dresses dressed the street, all at less than 60 euros a piece.

Karl Lagerfeld was no longer just a designer of luxury clothing. He had become a people's designer. "He would do better to tend his garden," mocked the two old men in the H&M advertisement. "Why tend your garden when you can have a forest?" was his reply. His wish to always see everything in big letters could not have been more clearly expressed: Coca-Cola, Volkswagen, Hogan, 3 Suisses, Sephora, Canderel; it is difficult to keep track of his collaborations.

Then came the campaign for road safety, launched in 2008, in which Karl sported a fluorescent high visibility jacket – thus joining the camp of those with a social conscience. The creative director at the advertising agency had been given the task of popularising the famous hi-vis jacket. He bought one and wore it himself for a whole day. "It's hideous," he heard from all sides. Like Margareta van den Bosch, he Googled three words: 'fashion+hideous+personality'. Lagerfeld's name popped up immediately. The creative director only had to make a small adjustment in Photoshop®, clothing the couturier in the celebrated jacket, above the baseline he had just thought up: "It's yellow, it's hideous, it doesn't go with anything, but it could save your life."

The Office of Road Safety is funded from the public purse. Only 4,000 euros were available to pay the model. "To Karl, zero or four thousand is pretty much the same," the couturier's assistant let slip. In the end, he posed for nothing. But Karl Lagerfeld gained much more than gratitude: his picture was posted on large panels, 4m x 3m, along all the motorways in France.

From then on, Kaiser Karl sought excess. John Galliano produced increasingly spectacular catwalk shows for Dior. Lagerfeld followed close behind. His clothes for Fendi appeared on the Great Wall of China in 2007. For Chanel, he built outsize sets at the Grand Palais: a reconstructed cruise ship, gardens in the French manner, the quays along the Seine and a rocket taking off in a cloud of smoke. Even improbable locations did not phase him: he completed the Paseo del Prado for four hundred VIPs in the heart of Havana in 2016. Thousands of Cubans swarmed the balconies, eager to catch a glimpse of the capitalist West, while the Chanel models paraded up and down. Every time doubts were expressed ("But that's going to cost a lot… It's going to shock them") Karl swept aside their fears: "Yes, but that's what's so amusing."

Luxury and bargains, beauty and kitsch; Karl Lagerfeld handled them all without fear, turn by turn. What couturier is capable of greater refinement in haute couture, while constantly celebrating himself with cheap trinkets? Karl Lagerfeld's effigy can be found on pins and badges in markets from Pekin to Moscow. All over the world, caps, tee shirts, mugs and pens bear his famous profile. The couturier lent his silhouette to teddy bears and Barbie dolls. Even Fendi created a 'Karlito' range, with a handbag and a key fob.

Was he happy, constantly wearing this mask? The question was superfluous; the mask had become him. "One day, you know," he laughed, "I went out in the street without dressing up, just in a cap. A guy stopped me after a few minutes: 'So, Karl, you're in disguise?'" His dark glasses, the ponytail, the dark suit and high white collar – his 'panoply' as he called it – had become his natural appearance, and his natural appearance was regarded as artificial.

Caroline de Monaco had been hounded by paparazzi for years – she was constantly amazed at the excitement Karl aroused. "I've made it my habit to make myself invisible," the Princess of Hanover assured me. "I can walk around Paris and no-one recognises me. When I'm with Karl, he's the one who gets mobbed."

Was this the global fame he sought? This representation of himself, perfectly stylised – dark glasses and ponytail – which gave him the celebrity of a rock star, transcending classes and generations? "One day, three young people from the suburbs stopped us in Rue de Rivoli, proclaiming: 'Ah, Karl, we love you!'" Jean-Jacques Picart, the famous fashion press attaché, told me. "They probably did not realise he was a fashion designer. But Lagerfeld was absolutely delighted. 'That's what I love,' he said, 'pleasing the young from every background.'"

Youth was an obsession with him, in this world where a model is reckoned to be too old for the job before she hits thirty. It was a challenge for Karl. He made a constant effort to remain at the furthest outpost of modernity. He bought several models of the latest smartphone every month and distributed them to his entourage. "I'm regenerating myself," he would say. The look he invented was perfect fodder for caricatures, but also for marketing in this new era of digital internet imagery, which spelt the end of the world he had known. In July 2013, he presented his Chanel catwalk show in the setting of a ruined theatre, with a science fiction city rising up in the background: what better way of saying he was still keen to adapt?

Karl Lagerfeld exercised complete control over almost everything that was written about him. He dominated the luxury trade for fifty years – and yet no biography has been written. Not in French, nor in English, nor in German. Most witnesses said nothing during his lifetime; if they did speak, it was under an oath of strict anonymity.

The star director of Chanel, the fashion house with a turnover of eight billion euros; the leading stylist at Fendi; at the heart of the world leader LVMH; friend of Bernard Arnault and the Wertheimer family – all of this was very important to the press and publishers. Negative reviews of the collections were very rare. There were few articles about Lagerfeld's career. In 2006, he led a court case against The Beautiful Fall, *a book describing thirty years of fashion in Paris, written by the British journalist Alicia Drake. He managed to get the French version redacted. Even better, by making it widely known in fashion circles that he detested the book, he managed – without lifting a finger – to stop fashion magazines from talking about it. Even today, many of his colleagues claim loudly and clearly not to have read it.*

"The media is easy to manipulate," he would say. His method was to offer himself up as a spectacle. His stock of anecdotes and biting comments was so large – even though he repeated them year after year – that most journalists gave up trying to investigate and just watched him on the screen. His appearance, his mittens, his rings, the way he drew his hair back in a ponytail – all of this drew their attention like a magnet. What better mask than a face everyone recognised?

17

By the end, Karl Lagerfeld considered himself immortal. In a world where everything is ephemeral and constantly renewing itself, there is no real end in sight. On a flight with his colleagues, the couturier would reassure those who prayed or grit their teeth at the first sign of turbulence: "Don't worry, nothing will happen to us because I'm here to live for ever." With his jeans, black jackets and the eighteenth-century black bow around his powdered ponytail, Kaiser Karl belonged to no historical period. Was he Ancien Régime or transhuman?

To cloud the issue further, he moved house again. The little kingdom of the Rue de l'Université, with its gilding and its candelabras, reminded him too much of bygone days. He chose three hundred and fifty square metres on Quai Voltaire, overlooking the Seine and the Louvre. The alterations lasted for two and a half years while the eight rooms were knocked together and everything was redecorated. The space was enormous and icily modern.

In the drawing room, retractable green-blue glass walls opened to reveal a bookcase containing a sample of the 40,000 books in his vast collection. "I don't want anything earlier than 2000," Lagerfeld told his decorator. IPod chargers, connected screens, large white leather sofas... A friend who came to visit him one evening was horrified to discover, in the chillingly clinical, chrome-filled kitchen, the designer's frugal dinner under a protective tinfoil sheet; it was waiting to be warmed up. He lived alone, apart from his staff, in this retreat that so closely matched his new state of mind.

Lagerfeld spent his mornings designing, "dressed in a large, white cotton piqué shirt," he reported, "powdered with talc and perfumed with Chanel N° 19" – a king whose body belongs to his subjects from the time he gets up to the time he goes to bed. In the afternoon, he scheduled fittings at Chanel or Studio KL, and press interviews. People were amazed that he accepted so many contracts over and above those that bound him to Chanel and Fendi, or that he should take up an invitation to open a hotel in Malaysia, or take part in advertising for fizzy drinks, cars or ice-creams; sullying his image and name. In truth, he struggled against anxiety and the void. His colleagues agreed to organise photo shoots or trips at the weekend, so that he always had something to do. At night, from the Quays, the windows of his apartment remained illuminated by halogen bulbs from dusk until dawn, as if for a child afraid of the dark.

The stylist had no offspring and no companion, except a pretty cat, a Burmese with celadon-green eyes. He sometimes took Choupette with him on his travels, in a Vuitton bag. When he left his ultra-modern living quarters, the animal's nurse sent pictures of Choupette to his phone at regular intervals. Choupette, lording it over the designs for the next collection. Choupette, asleep with her doll, Karl, like a faithful, all-consumed lover. With no thought of causing a shock, in those times of financial crisis and social disruption, Karl made it widely known that, thanks to the advertising photos in which the cat appeared, this charming moggie was worth three million euros and had already been written into his will. Karl even took a photograph of himself as a plaything between the paws of this small feline, in ironic reference to himself.

After the emancipation of the 1950s, the wild partying of the 1970s, success and admiration, Karl Lagerfeld quietly prepared himself for his final lonely journey. There was no-one around him of the same age. They had gradually disappeared, or else he had turned them out. He was of the opinion that the 'elderly' were too quick to give up competitive life in the world. He gave up nothing. One day he was watching a German documentary about people who had reached the age of 100 and was struck by something he had already been thinking about. The documentary makers were trying to find the secret of longevity: food, sport, sleep? "I'm always curious about what will happen tomorrow," said a stylish old lady of 106. That was exactly it. "I want to know everything, to understand everything, be up to date with everything," Karl said. "It's a kind of intellectual opportunism, a frivolous frenzy, superficial perhaps, but at the end of the day, I am better educated, more cultivated than most of the people who do this job."

Karl used the enormous floor-to-ceiling bookcase at the back of the library he had created in Rue de Lille in Paris as a backdrop for his photographic studio. In it could be found poetry, art books, dictionaries in Greek and Italian, history books and literature in French, English and German. Colette, Catherine Pozzi, Emily Dickinson and Keyserling were his favourite writers, but he also owned various versions of Faust, the tale of the man who sold his soul to the devil in exchange for universal knowledge. Faust was him: living to eternity.

In photographs, access to which was strictly controlled, the couturier is always surrounded by young people. In 2008, Karl launched a young male model, a first among the female beauties whose careers he had created. Baptiste Giabiconi had a look reminiscent of Karl in his twenties. Dark brown eyes, sensual mouth and the same Middle-Eastern features that caused confusion, making people think Lagerfeld was from the shores of the Bosporus, rather than a town between the North Sea and the Baltic. A foolish rumour had it that Karl was in love with the boy, born in 1989, the year when Jacques de Bascher died. In fact, he had confusedly recognised his physical double in this young man who called him 'papa'.

Other members of this small reconstituted family (which he publicised in short, finely honed films for Chanel) included the model Brad Kroenig and, in particular, Brad's son, Hudson. As Lagerfeld's godson, he was quite the Little Lord Fauntleroy: beautiful to look at and badly brought up. As with Choupette, Karl made sure that the small boy was spoilt rotten. "I gave him a Rolex because he complained of always being late for school," Lagerfeld notes in his journal, without fear of causing outrage. Such was his way of defying convention.

The man he chose for company and as a confidant, the man he dined with every evening to relieve his solitude, was the diametric opposite of this little nine-year-old prince. Sébastien Jondeau was a handsome young man, intelligent and upright. He would always be seen a few steps away from the couturier, protecting him from the touch of beggars, opportunists and fans. 'Seb', as he was called at the Kaiser's court, was fifteen years old when, working in his godfather's removals business during the holidays, he was employed to load Lagerfeld's furniture and paintings into a lorry. He had never seen a mansion to compare with the house on Rue de l'Université, nor a client to compare with this one: half-aristocrat, half-punk, handing out tips of 500 euros. When Sébastien reached the age of twenty-one, Karl hired him as his bodyguard and, basically, odd-job man.

Their story is the outcome of two worlds coming together – and in Lagerfeld's eyes, a successful educational exchange. Jondeau grew up between Aubervilliers and Garges-lès-Gonesse. "When we used to go to take a private plane from Le Bourget, in Karl's Rolls, we would pass the council block where I used to live, and the fields where I used to ride stolen motor bikes," he told me. Jondeau learned to recognise, in Lagerfeld's strange milieu, "the people who clothed people and the people who saved people, and also the two or three people we had to manage." The couturier employed him, housed him close to his own flat, and used him both in advertising films and on the catwalk. As Jondeau said, "He gave me education and books, brought me history and art on a plate." Perhaps in the evening, Kaiser Karl unveiled his real character to him, as one would loosen the strings of a puppet? "He had no secret life," the bodyguard assured me. "His life was like a monk's life; he only worked." Lagerfeld was a boss and a father at the same time – "but also a child and a friend," said 'Seb', who saw everything but took care not to notice Lagerfeld when necessary, giving the couturier his privacy.

Life could have continued in this vein. A few society dinners with Bernard Arnault where Lagerfeld met Emmanuel and Brigitte Macron. Travel all over the world, endless interviews. Spectacular catwalk shows and crowds of stars.

Then, one day, Karl Lagerfeld learned that he was ill. "Cancer," said the doctors in the American Hospital. Cancer was not AIDS, back when Jacques first realised he was infected. You could recover from cancer. Lagerfeld had read how François Mitterand lived with his cancer for fourteen years, in spite of the prognosis – and, like him, he decided to conceal it. Even Sébastien, who accompanied him to every medical appointment or to the acupuncturist; even Caroline Lebar, his most loyal colleague; guessed more than they knew. One day Caroline was describing the tests a friend of hers had taken for suspected prostate cancer. Lagerfeld calmly asked, "What is his PSA count?" It was at that moment Caroline realised he was perfectly well informed on the subject.

Lagerfeld had to resort to some subterfuge when the metastases took over. He had adopted the habit of coming to greet the crowd at the end of a fashion show, supported on little Hudson's shoulder to stop himself falling. His worst fear was tripping in public on the catwalk – the backdrop to his private life. His bones had become brittle. He was always under fire from photographers, in an era that instantly records itself on Instagram; worrying pictures had been published showing him smiling without teeth. His team had to allege an allergy to anaesthetics to explain why he had not attended to his dental needs.

In January 2018, at the age of eighty-five, when Karl appeared sporting a well-trimmed white beard that hardly concealed his pale lips, the change was so palpable that he had to go on television to certify he was in good health. This was a trap, for a man who had created an appearance for himself that identified him all over the world. A few years earlier, Lagerfeld had said with his usual self-deprecating irony: "Every morning, I take a quarter of an hour to style myself. I prepare the puppet." Now, that puppet was more crucial than ever. Lagerfeld had to continuously don the mask of a man full of energy, when every day he felt more enfeebled.

In 2015, his friends had all seen the way he had run away rather than confront death when his friend Pierre

Hebey, a lawyer and essayist, was knocked down by a car. Formerly sparkling with intelligence, Hebey was now no more than a shadow of himself. So, Karl had removed himself from his circle. He sold his house in the Basque country, which he had initially bought for its proximity to his lawyer's home, and lost his temper with Geneviève, Hebey's wife. In fact, he organised his life so as to put a salutary distance between himself and his old friend, as if escaping the evil eye.

This cowardice, or possibly this denial, was incurable, and it never left Lagerfeld. In spring 2018, Delphine Arnault presented the LVMH prize, awarded every year to young designers. Karl Lagerfeld had been president of the jury since its inception, as a tutelary figure. Delphine had always been shy, although she had inherited a fortune as Arnault's eldest daughter, and was the assistant director of Louis Vuitton. It was as though she was crushed by her all-powerful father, who made all the decisions about the future of the Group and his children. With his experience as a solitary child, Lagerfeld took her under his wing. "We need to choose the ones who, in ten years' time, will be amongst the top achievers in fashion," she said, to open the jury's deliberation. The assembled company heard that famous voice cry out in its German accent: "In ten years' time? But we'll still be here!"

What will remain of Karl Lagerfeld? Clothes? They are so ephemeral. A style? Did he really have one, acting as he did as a mercenary for other fashion houses, not his own? Thousands of drawings? A legendary life?

"I only sell the façade; personal truth is for myself alone," Lagerfeld often used to say. He survived fashion, survived its industrialisation, survived his rival Saint Laurent and even Pierre Bergé, who died a year and a half before him without making peace. A man for all seasons, he surfed the superficial, never letting the acid of celebrity attack his exterior. This is the domain in which he was probably most successful. Known everywhere, rich and perfectly alone. He was the last emperor in the kingdom he chose for himself. Kaiser Karl.

Acknowledgements

From Hamburg to New York, from Paris to Monaco, from couture workshops to nightclubs, many of the people who knew Karl Lagerfeld have kept me company during this investigation.

He talked a lot himself, often re-inventing his past; reconstructing the periods he lived through has not been the least of my difficulties. The couturier's quotations often come from the many interviews he gave to the press, but also from a long interview he granted me in July 2018 for a series of articles published in *Le Monde* that August; these all gave me the desire to pursue the story and develop it.

From among those who shared their memories of Karl Lagerfeld, I am particularly grateful to:

Philippe Aghion, Jean-Jacques Aillagon, Thierry Ardisson, Bernard Arnault, Antoine Arnault, Delphine Arnault, Diane de Beauvau-Craon, Anita Briey, Victoire de Castellane, Claude Chirac, Marie-Louise de Clermont-Tonnerre, Vincent Darré, Gilles Dufour, Inès de la Fressange, Philippe Heurtault, Patrick Hourcade, Camille Hutin, Sébastien Jondeau, Claude Lalanne, Sophie de Langlade, Caroline Lebar, Suzy Menkes, Her Royal Highness Princess Caroline of Monaco, Philippe Morillon, Florentine Pabst, Paquita Paquin, Bruno Pawlowski, Jean-Jacques Picard, François Pinault, Eric Pfrunder, Jacques Polge, Loïc Prigent, Colombe Pringle, Nathalie Rykiel, Ursula Scheube, Corey Tippin, Céline Toledano, Ralph Toledano, Laurent Toulouse, Virginie Viard, Christoph von Weyhe.

I should also like to thank the seamstresses at Chanel who were kind enough to allow me to penetrate their marvellous workshops, and answered my many questions. Finally, my publisher Alexandre Wickham, whose enthusiasm and friendship have been so valuable to me during the writing of this book.

Bibliography

Some of the books and documentary films that have enlightened me on the world of fashion, the fashion industry and its culture:

WORKS

The Beautiful Fall: Fashion, Genius and Glorious Excess in 1970s Paris, Alicia Drake, Bloomsbury, 2007.
Merci Karl! Arnaud Maillard, Calman-Levy, 2007.
Le Monde selon Karl, Jean-Christophe Napias et Patrick Mauriès, Flammarion, 2013.
Jacques de Bascher: Éloge de la chute, Philippe Heurtault, Éditions Michel de Maule, 2017.
Jacques de Bascher: Dandy de l'ombre, Marie Ottavi, Séguier, 2017.

DOCUMENTARIES

Lagerfeld confidentiel, Rodolphe Marconi et Liova Jedlicki, 2007.
Karl Lagerfeld, un roi seul, Thierry Demaizière et Alban Teurlai, collection "Empreinte", France 5, 2008.
Inès de la Fressange: "En avant, calme et droit !", Jean-François Boyer et Gaëlle Le Fur, 2010.
Karl Lagerfeld se dessine, Loïc Prigent, 2012.

OTHER BOOKS BY RAPHAËLLE BACQUÉ

Chirac président, les coulisses d'une victoire, with Denis Saverot, Éditions du Rocher/DBW, 1995.
Chirac ou le démon du pouvoir, Albin Michel, 2002.
La Femme fatale, with Ariane Chemin, Albin Michel, 2007.
L'Enfer de Matignon, Albin Michel, 2008.
Le Dernier Mort de Mitterrand, Grasset, 2010.
Les Strauss-Kahn, with Ariane Chemin, Albin Michel, 2012.
Richie, Grasset, 2015.
La Communauté, with Ariane Chemin, Albin Michel, 2018.